MATH Perplexors

DEDUCTIVE LOGIC PUZZLES

MindWare®

® brainy toys for kids of all ages®

www.MINDWAREonline.com

A MindWare® Original!

Our entire selection of Brainy Toys for Kids of All Ages® is available at www.MINDWAREonline.com, or by calling us at 800-999-0398 to request a catalog.

Coloring Books

Each of our coloring books offer one of a kind patterns, textures and styles you make your own by choosing how to bring them to life.

Animal Habitats Series

Creature Camouflage Series

Designs Series

Lights Series

Modern Patterns Series

Mosaics Series

Quilts Series

Scapes Series

Transformations Series

Puzzle Books

Our puzzle books build skills in many areas—from logic to math, spatial reasoning to verbal skills.

Addition Adventures

Analogy Challenges

Clip Clues

Code Breakers

Deducibles

Directive Detective

Division Designs

Fast Fact Trivia

Grid Perplexors

Logic Links

Math Path Puzzles

Math Perplexors

More Multiplication Mosaics

Multiplication Mosaics

Noodlers

Number Junctions

Perplexors

Sequencers

Subtraction Secrets

Tactic Twisters

Tan-Tastic Tangrams

Venn Perplexors

Word Winks

Word Wise

Games and Activities

Building blocks to strategic games, mystery puzzles to imaginative play — enhance abstract thinking and reasoning skills with our ingenious games and activities.

Bella's Mystery Decks

Blik-Blok

Block Buddies

Chaos

Cross-Eyed

Flip 4

Gambit

Hue Knew?

Logic Links Game

Make Your Own Mask Kit

Noodlers Game

Pattern Play

Qwirkle

Tally Rally

Squzzles

Configure nine 3 x 3 pieces into a square where all images match up on every single side. Three challenging puzzles per box.

3-D Scramblers

Animal Babies

Creature Kingdom

Creepy Crawlers

Illusions

Insect Infested

Nocturnal Animals

Optical Illusions

Play Ball!

Wings & Wheels

World Money

7/2007

Individual Puzzles by Greg Gottstein
Editing by Eric Benjamin and Sheila Hatche
Design by Kristine Mudd

EAN 978-1-933054-64-3
SKU 36028

MindWare®
brainy toys for kids of all ages®

for other MindWare products visit our website
www.MINDWAREonline.com

Instructions

When you are faced with a number of options, logic is often used to make a choice. Logic uses reasoning and proof to help you analyze information and come to a conclusion.

All the information needed to solve a Math Perplexors logic problem is given in the puzzle story and its following clues. In the beginning, all the possibilities are listed for each category. As they are eliminated by information given in the clues, these possibilities should be crossed off. In a vertical column, if all the answers in a column are eliminated except for one, then that one remaining possibility must be the answer and it should be circled. The same is true in horizontal rows. If all the possibilities are eliminated in a row except for one, then that one remaining possibility must be the answer and it should be circled.

Perhaps the easiest way to understand this technique is to look at the sample puzzle and follow along as the reasons for crossing off and circling an answer is given.

THE STORY

Three geckos named Greg, Gail, and Gordon lived together in the desert. They were 8, 4, and 2 years old. One recent day they ate 40, 20, and 10 flies for dinner. Based on the clues, match geckos with their ages and fly consumptions.

THE CLUES

1. Multiply Greg's age by 10 and the answer is the number of flies he ate for dinner.
2. Gail ate twice as many flies as the oldest gecko.

Greg	Gail	Gordon
~~8 years old~~	8 years old	8 years old
4 years old	4 years old	4 years old
2 years old	2 years old	2 years old
40 flies	40 flies	40 flies
20 flies	20 flies	20 flies
~~10 flies~~	10 flies	10 flies

Clue 1 allows you to cross out 8 years old under Greg because 10 x 8 = 80 and 80 is not a choice. Clue 1 also allows you to cross out 10 flies under Greg because multiplying 10 by any age number cannot result in 10.

Greg	Gail	Gordon
~~8 years old~~	~~8 years old~~	(8 years old)
4 years old	4 years old	~~4 years old~~
2 years old	2 years old	~~2 years old~~
40 flies	40 flies	~~40 flies~~
20 flies	20 flies	~~20 flies~~
~~10 flies~~	~~10 flies~~	(10 flies)

Clue 2 allows you to cross-out 8 years old under Gail as she ate twice as many flies as the 8 year old gecko. This means Gordon must be the 8 year old gecko and that number should be circled under Gordon, and 4 years old and 2 years old under Gordon should be crossed off the list. Clue 2 also allows you to cross out 10 flies under Gail as 10 is not twice as much as anything on the list. Crossing off 10 under Gail means that Gordon had to be the gecko that ate 10 flies. 10 flies under Gordon should be circled, and 40 flies and 20 flies under Gordon should be crossed off.

Greg	Gail	Gordon
~~8 years old~~	~~8 years old~~	(8 years old)
(4 years old)	~~4 years old~~	~~4 years old~~
~~2 years old~~	(2 years old)	~~2 years old~~
(40 flies)	~~40 flies~~	~~40 flies~~
~~20 flies~~	(20 flies)	~~20 flies~~
~~10 flies~~	~~10 flies~~	(10 flies)

Now that we know Gordon is the oldest gecko and he ate 10 flies, and we know that Gail ate 20 flies because she ate twice as many flies as Gordon. Circle 20 flies under Gail and complete the crossing out; we know that Greg ate 40 flies.

Clue 1 says multiplying Greg's age by 10 reveals the number of flies he ate. Since we now know he ate 40 flies, we must conclude he is 4 years old because 4 x 10=40.

1 Timely Crows

THE STORY

Punky, Hinky and Pecky were three crows living in three different trees in the Fridley forest. The trees were 100, 90 and 80 feet tall. They spent exactly six hours a day sleeping but split the remaining 18 hours doing exactly the same three tasks. However, none of the three crows spent exactly the same amount of time on a task as another crow. They spent 8, 6 and 4 hours eating scraps. They spent 8, 6 and 4 hours raiding Farmer Brown's cornfields. They spent 8, 6 and 4 hours chasing owls. Based on the clues, match the crows with the heights of their trees, and the amount of time they spent eating scraps, raiding cornfields and chasing owls.

THE CLUES

1. Punky and Hinky spent a combined total of 10 hours eating scraps.
2. Hinky and Pecky spent a combined total of 10 hours chasing owls.
3. Hinky spent the least amount of time eating scraps.
4. If you divided Pecky's tree height number by his scraps number, the answer would be 10.
5. Punky's tree was exactly 10 feet taller than Pecky's tree.

Punky	Hinky	Pecky
100 feet 90 feet 80 feet	100 feet 90 feet 80 feet	100 feet 90 feet 80 feet
8 hrs. eating 6 hrs. eating 4 hrs. eating	8 hrs. eating 6 hrs. eating 4 hrs. eating	8 hrs. eating 6 hrs. eating 4 hrs. eating
8 hrs. raiding 6 hrs. raiding 4 hrs. raiding	8 hrs. raiding 6 hrs. raiding 4 hrs. raiding	8 hrs. raiding 6 hrs. raiding 4 hrs. raiding
8 hrs. chasing 6 hrs. chasing 4 hrs. chasing	8 hrs. chasing 6 hrs. chasing 4 hrs. chasing	8 hrs. chasing 6 hrs. chasing 4 hrs. chasing

2 Going Bananas

THE STORY

Bunky, Billy and Blinky were three gorillas living together in the Rainiere rainforest. They were 30, 25 and 20 years old. Recently, they each received a shipment of 200 bananas, and they used their bananas in three different ways. They used 100, 75 and 25 bananas to make banana cream pies. They used 100, 75 and 25 bananas to make banana jelly. They used 100, 75 and 25 bananas to make banana pudding. Based on the clues, match the gorillas with their ages, and the number of their 200 bananas they each used to make pies, jelly and pudding.

THE CLUES

1. Bunky made 3 pies for each year of his life, and Billy made 5 pies for each year of his life.
2. Billy used more bananas making jelly than Bunky.

Bunky	Billy	Blinky
30 years old 25 years old 20 years old	30 years old 25 years old 20 years old	30 years old 25 years old 20 years old
100 pies 75 pies 25 pies	100 pies 75 pies 25 pies	100 pies 75 pies 25 pies
100 jelly 75 jelly 25 jelly	100 jelly 75 jelly 25 jelly	100 jelly 75 jelly 25 jelly
100 pudding 75 pudding 25 pudding	100 pudding 75 pudding 25 pudding	100 pudding 75 pudding 25 pudding

3 Fruit Counts

THE STORY

Sharon, Sammy, Sarah and Sherman each were the proud owners of four different fruit trees. They each owned a peach tree, an apple tree, a lemon tree and a pear tree. One year, they decided to count the fruit they received from each tree and compare the results with each other. By an amazing coincidence they all recorded receiving exactly 2,500 pieces of fruit from their four trees. Nobody in their orchards had trees that produced exactly the same amount of any type of fruit in that orchard, and nobody had a tree that produced the same amount of fruit as any of his or her other trees. The peach trees produced 1,000, 750, 500 and 250 peaches. The apple trees produced 1,000, 750, 500 and 250 apples. The lemon trees produced 1,000, 750, 500 and 250 lemons. The pear trees produced 1,000, 750, 500 and 250 pears. Based on the clues, match the names with the amount of peaches, apples, lemons and pears their trees produced.

THE CLUES

1. Sarah and Sherman's lemon trees provided them with a total of 750 lemons, and their apple trees provided them with a combined total of 750 apples.
2. Add Sharon's number of peaches to Sarah's number of lemons to discover Sammy's number of peaches.
3. Sherman's peach tree produced more peaches than Sarah's peach tree, and Sammy's lemon tree produced the most lemons.

Sharon	Sammy	Sarah	Sherman
1,000 peaches	1,000 peaches	1,000 peaches	1,000 peaches
750 peaches	750 peaches	750 peaches	750 peaches
500 peaches	500 peaches	500 peaches	500 peaches
250 peaches	250 peaches	250 peaches	250 peaches
1,000 apples	1,000 apples	1,000 apples	1,000 apples
750 apples	750 apples	750 apples	750 apples
500 apples	500 apples	500 apples	500 apples
250 apples	250 apples	250 apples	250 apples
1,000 lemons	1,000 lemons	1,000 lemons	1,000 lemons
750 lemons	750 lemons	750 lemons	750 lemons
500 lemons	500 lemons	500 lemons	500 lemons
250 lemons	250 lemons	250 lemons	250 lemons
1,000 pears	1,000 pears	1,000 pears	1,000 pears
750 pears	750 pears	750 pears	750 pears
500 pears	500 pears	500 pears	500 pears
250 pears	250 pears	250 pears	250 pears

4 At Home With A Squirrel

THE STORY

Nutter, Buffy, Sammy and Louie each made their homes in a different hollow tree in the forest. The trees were 150, 100, 75 and 50 years old. The diameters of the trees were 80, 60, 40 and 30 inches. The trees were 110, 100, 90 and 50 feet in height. The squirrels had been busy gathering nuts for the winter season and had gathered 1,500, 1,000, 800 and 600 nuts. Based on the clues, match the squirrels with the age, diameter and height of their trees, and the number of nuts they gathered.

THE CLUES

1. The diameter of Nutter's tree was the same as the radius of Louie's tree, and the radius of Sammy's tree was the same as the diameter of Buffy's tree.
2. Multiply Nutter's radius by 5 to find the age of Buffy's tree, and multiply Buffy's radius by 5 to find the age of Nutter's tree.
3. Multiply the age of Louie's tree by 2 to determine the age of Buffy's tree.
4. The combined height of Sammy and Louie's trees was 70 yards, and Nutter's tree was 20 yards shorter than Louie's tree.
5. Sammy and Louie's combined nut total was 1,400 nuts, and Buffy and Louie's combined nut total was 2,100 nuts.

Nutter	Buffy	Sammy	Louie
150 years old	150 years old	150 years old	150 years old
100 years old	100 years old	100 years old	100 years old
75 years old	75 years old	75 years old	75 years old
50 years old	50 years old	50 years old	50 years old
80 in. diameter	80 in. diameter	80 in. diameter	80 in. diameter
60 in. diameter	60 in. diameter	60 in. diameter	60 in. diameter
40 in. diameter	40 in. diameter	40 in. diameter	40 in. diameter
30 in. diameter	30 in. diameter	30 in. diameter	30 in. diameter
110 feet tall	110 feet tall	110 feet tall	110 feet tall
100 feet tall	100 feet tall	100 feet tall	100 feet tall
90 feet tall	90 feet tall	90 feet tall	90 feet tall
50 feet tall	50 feet tall	50 feet tall	50 feet tall
1,500 nuts	1,500 nuts	1,500 nuts	1,500 nuts
1,000 nuts	1,000 nuts	1,000 nuts	1,000 nuts
800 nuts	800 nuts	800 nuts	800 nuts
600 nuts	600 nuts	600 nuts	600 nuts

5 Your Turtles Are Numbered

THE STORY

Tara, Tilly, Tammy and Thomas were four turtles living together in the Glenview pond. These four turtles fell passionately in love with the numbers 5, 10, 15 and 20, and insisted upon wearing all four numbers every day on the four items of clothing they wore every day. Each item of clothing would bear one of these four numbers so they could wear all four numbers all the time. The turtles always wore a hat, a vest, a shirt and a pair of shorts with a different favorite number on these clothes. Trouble developed when a turtle wore the same number on the same item of clothing as another turtle wore on the same day. To ensure peace, the turtles worked out a daily schedule so that all the turtles could wear all four favorite numbers but no turtle would wear the same number on the same item of clothing as another turtle did on that day. Based on the clues, see if you can figure out today's schedule.

THE CLUES

1. Multiply Tammy's hat number by 2 to identify Thomas' hat number.
2. Subtract Tilly's hat number from Tara's hat number to determine Tilly's vest number.
3. Tara did not wear 15 on her vest or shirt that day, and Tilly did not wear 10 on her shorts that day.
4. Tammy did not wear 15 on her vest, and Thomas did not wear 20 on his hat that day.

Tara	Tilly	Tammy	Thomas
5 hat	5 hat	5 hat	5 hat
10 hat	10 hat	10 hat	10 hat
15 hat	15 hat	15 hat	15 hat
20 hat	20 hat	20 hat	20 hat
5 vest	5 vest	5 vest	5 vest
10 vest	10 vest	10 vest	10 vest
15 vest	15 vest	15 vest	15 vest
20 vest	20 vest	20 vest	20 vest
5 shirt	5 shirt	5 shirt	5 shirt
10 shirt	10 shirt	10 shirt	10 shirt
15 shirt	15 shirt	15 shirt	15 shirt
20 shirt	20 shirt	20 shirt	20 shirt
5 shorts	5 shorts	5 shorts	5 shorts
10 shorts	10 shorts	10 shorts	10 shorts
15 shorts	15 shorts	15 shorts	15 shorts
20 shorts	20 shorts	20 shorts	20 shorts

6 Too Much Work?

THE STORY

The Towns of Glenview, Northbrook, Northfield and Deerfield took a census of the four most common occupations of their citizens. The four most common occupations were doctors, lawyers, teachers and florists. There were 6,000, 5,000, 4,000 and 3,500 doctors. There were 8,000, 7,500, 7,000 and 6,000 lawyers. There were 4,700, 4,600, 4,000 and 3,000 teachers. There were 5,000, 4,500, 4,300 and 4,200 florists. Based on the clues, match the towns with the number of doctors, lawyers, teachers and florists who lived in those towns.

THE CLUES

1. Each town had the most of one of the four occupations, but each town also had the fewest of one of the four occupations.
2. Northfield and Deerfield had a combined total of 10,000 doctors and 13,000 lawyers.
3. Northbrook and Northfield had a combined total of 9,000 doctors and 15,000 lawyers.
4. Northfield had more teachers than Deerfield.
5. Northbrook had exactly 200 more florists than Deerfield, and Deerfield had more teachers than Glenview.

Glenview	Northbrook	Northfield	Deerfield
6,000 doctors	6,000 doctors	6,000 doctors	6,000 doctors
5,000 doctors	5,000 doctors	5,000 doctors	5,000 doctors
4,000 doctors	4,000 doctors	4,000 doctors	4,000 doctors
3,500 doctors	3,500 doctors	3,500 doctors	3,500 doctors
8,000 lawyers	8,000 lawyers	8,000 lawyers	8,000 lawyers
7,500 lawyers	7,500 lawyers	7,500 lawyers	7,500 lawyers
7,000 lawyers	7,000 lawyers	7,000 lawyers	7,000 lawyers
6,000 lawyers	6,000 lawyers	6,000 lawyers	6,000 lawyers
4,700 teachers	4,700 teachers	4,700 teachers	4,700 teachers
4,600 teachers	4,600 teachers	4,600 teachers	4,600 teachers
4,000 teachers	4,000 teachers	4,000 teachers	4,000 teachers
3,000 teachers	3,000 teachers	3,000 teachers	3,000 teachers
5,000 florists	5,000 florists	5,000 florists	5,000 florists
4,500 florists	4,500 florists	4,500 florists	4,500 florists
4,300 florists	4,300 florists	4,300 florists	4,300 florists
4,200 florists	4,200 florists	4,200 florists	4,200 florists

7 Watching Robins

THE STORY

Four robins named Romeo, Richie, Robbie and Ruth were dedicated people watchers. They loved counting the number of men, women, boys and girls they saw as they went worming about their day. One recent day, they got together and compared their people watching totals for that day. They reported seeing 400, 375, 300 and 275 men, and 750, 700, 600 and 550 women. They reported seeing 2,200, 2,100, 2,000 and 1,750 boys, and 2,300, 2,000, 1,950 and 1,925 girls. Based on the clues, match the robins with the number of men, women, boys and girls they reported seeing that day.

THE CLUES

1. Romeo and Richie had the sharpest eyes and one of them saw the most of two of the four groups, and the other saw the most of the remaining two of the four groups.
2. Robbie and Ruth were the worst people watchers, and one of them saw the fewest of two of the four groups and the other saw the fewest of the remaining two of the four groups.
3. Romeo and Richie saw a combined total of 4,300 boys and 4,300 girls.
4. Robbie saw exactly 100 fewer men than Romeo, and Ruth saw exactly 100 fewer men than Richie.
5. Robbie did not see the fewest women or girls, and Richie did not see the most women or boys.
6. Robbie saw fewer women than Richie.

Romeo	Richie	Robbie	Ruth
400 men	400 men	400 men	400 men
375 men	375 men	375 men	375 men
300 men	300 men	300 men	300 men
275 men	275 men	275 men	275 men
750 women	750 women	750 women	750 women
700 women	700 women	700 women	700 women
600 women	600 women	600 women	600 women
550 women	550 women	550 women	550 women
2,200 boys	2,200 boys	2,200 boys	2,200 boys
2,100 boys	2,100 boys	2,100 boys	2,100 boys
2,000 boys	2,000 boys	2,000 boys	2,000 boys
1,750 boys	1,750 boys	1,750 boys	1,750 boys
2,300 girls	2,300 girls	2,300 girls	2,300 girls
2,000 girls	2,000 girls	2,000 girls	2,000 girls
1,950 girls	1,950 girls	1,950 girls	1,950 girls
1,925 girls	1,925 girls	1,925 girls	1,925 girls

8 Farming Figures

THE STORY

Four farmers named Smith, Jones, Brown and White all had farms of exactly 525 acres. The farms were all divided exactly the same. Each farm had a 200-acre plot, a 150-acre plot, a 100-acre plot and a 75-acre plot. The farmers all planted exactly the same four crops: wheat, corn, soybeans and beets. However, the farmers all had different opinions about how much acreage to devote to each crop, and no farmer devoted the same amount of acreage to each crop as any other farmer. Based on the clues, match the farmers with the acres they devoted to each crop.

THE CLUES

1. Farmers Brown and White planted a combined total of 175 acres of wheat and 175 acres of corn.
2. Farmers Jones and Brown planted a combined total of 300 acres of wheat.
3. Farmers Smith and Brown planted a combined total of 300 acres of soybeans.

Smith	Jones	Brown	White
200 wheat	200 wheat	200 wheat	200 wheat
150 wheat	150 wheat	150 wheat	150 wheat
100 wheat	100 wheat	100 wheat	100 wheat
75 wheat	75 wheat	75 wheat	75 wheat
200 corn	200 corn	200 corn	200 corn
150 corn	150 corn	150 corn	150 corn
100 corn	100 corn	100 corn	100 corn
75 corn	75 corn	75 corn	75 corn
200 soybeans	200 soybeans	200 soybeans	200 soybeans
150 soybeans	150 soybeans	150 soybeans	150 soybeans
100 soybeans	100 soybeans	100 soybeans	100 soybeans
75 soybeans	75 soybeans	75 soybeans	75 soybeans
200 beets	200 beets	200 beets	200 beets
150 beets	150 beets	150 beets	150 beets
100 beets	100 beets	100 beets	100 beets
75 beets	75 beets	75 beets	75 beets

9 I Get A Kick Out Of You

THE STORY

Ryan, Reggie, Rosa and Ruby were four players on the Springfield soccer team. Their uniform numbers were 90, 80, 75 and 40. They kept a record of how many times they had been kicked instead of the ball during the soccer season and compared their results. They had been kicked in the shin bone 500, 490, 470 and 450 times. They had been kicked in the ankle 325, 320, 315 and 300 times. They had been kicked in the head 77, 74, 71 and 65 times. Based on the clues, match the players with their uniform numbers and the number of times they had been kicked in the shin, ankle and head.

THE CLUES

1. If you multiplied Ryan's uniform number by 10, the answer would be the same as the combined total of times he was kicked in the shin and ankle.
2. If you added Ruby's uniform number to the number of times she was kicked in the shin, the answer would be the number of times Reggie was kicked in the shin.
3. Rosa did not have the highest uniform number, and Rosa was kicked in the ankle more than Reggie but less than Ruby.
4. Ruby was kicked in the head exactly 3 fewer times than Rosa, and Ryan was kicked in the head exactly 3 fewer times than Ruby.

Ryan	Reggie	Rosa	Ruby
90 uniform	90 uniform	90 uniform	90 uniform
80 uniform	80 uniform	80 uniform	80 uniform
75 uniform	75 uniform	75 uniform	75 uniform
40 uniform	40 uniform	40 uniform	40 uniform
500 shin	500 shin	500 shin	500 shin
490 shin	490 shin	490 shin	490 shin
470 shin	470 shin	470 shin	470 shin
450 shin	450 shin	450 shin	450 shin
325 ankle	325 ankle	325 ankle	325 ankle
320 ankle	320 ankle	320 ankle	320 ankle
315 ankle	315 ankle	315 ankle	315 ankle
300 ankle	300 ankle	300 ankle	300 ankle
77 head	77 head	77 head	77 head
74 head	74 head	74 head	74 head
71 head	71 head	71 head	71 head
65 head	65 head	65 head	65 head

10 And The Winner Is

THE STORY

Tom, Tess, Tillie and Timmy were all candidates for the office of mayor of Hamilton. They were 65, 60, 50 and 45 years old. During the campaign they made 5,000, 4,900, 4,700 and 4,500 speeches. They spent $30,000, $27,000, $25,000 and $20,000 on their campaigns. They received 20,000, 18,000, 17,000 and 15,000 votes. Based on the clues, match the candidates with their ages, their number of speeches, the money they spent, and the votes they received.

THE CLUES

1. Multiply Tom's age by 500 to reveal how much money he spent, but multiply Tillie's age by 500 to uncover how much money she spent.
2. Multiply Timmy's age by 100 to determine the number of speeches Tom gave, and multiply Tillie's age by 100 to identify the number of speeches Timmy gave.
3. Tillie gave more speeches than Tess.
4. The candidate who spent the most money received the fewest votes.
5. Tom spent more than Tillie.
6. The youngest candidate spent the least amount of money.
7. Neither the oldest candidate nor the youngest candidate received the most votes.
8. Tess received exactly 3,000 fewer votes than Tillie.

Tom	Tess	Tillie	Timmy
65 years old	65 years old	65 years old	65 years old
60 years old	60 years old	60 years old	60 years old
50 years old	50 years old	50 years old	50 years old
45 years old	45 years old	45 years old	45 years old
5,000 speeches	5,000 speeches	5,000 speeches	5,000 speeches
4,900 speeches	4,900 speeches	4,900 speeches	4,900 speeches
4,700 speeches	4,700 speeches	4,700 speeches	4,700 speeches
4,500 speeches	4,500 speeches	4,500 speeches	4,500 speeches
$30,000	$30,000	$30,000	$30,000
$27,000	$27,000	$27,000	$27,000
$25,000	$25,000	$25,000	$25,000
$20,000	$20,000	$20,000	$20,000
20,000 votes	20,000 votes	20,000 votes	20,000 votes
18,000 votes	18,000 votes	18,000 votes	18,000 votes
17,000 votes	17,000 votes	17,000 votes	17,000 votes
15,000 votes	15,000 votes	15,000 votes	15,000 votes

11 The School Is Jumping

THE STORY

Every year the Stanton School holds a field day when it chooses the best competitors in three Olympic events chosen at random. This year, the three events were the running broad jump, the shot put and the pole vault. Glenn, Gloria, Gina, George and Gail were the top five competitors in these three events. They broad jumped 18, 17, 16, 13 and 12 feet. They threw the shot put 40, 39, 37, 35 and 30 feet. They pole vaulted 16, 15, 14, 13 and 12 feet. Based on the clues, match the competitors with their scores in the three events.

THE CLUES

1. Glenn, Gloria and George each won one of the three events.
2. Glenn, Gina and Gail each had the lowest score in one of the three events.
3. Glenn and George's combined broad jump total was exactly 10 yards.
4. In the pole vault, Gina jumped exactly 2 feet higher than Gail and exactly 1 foot higher than George.
5. Glenn pole vaulted exactly 1 foot higher than Gina.
6. Multiply Gloria's broad jump number by 3 to acquire her shot put number.
7. Gina broad jumped 1 yard more than Gloria.
8. George, of course, threw the shot put farther than Gail.

Glenn	Gloria	Gina	George	Gail
18 ft. broad	18 ft. broad	18 ft. broad	18 ft. broad	18 ft. broad
17 ft. broad	17 ft. broad	17 ft. broad	17 ft. broad	17 ft. broad
16 ft. broad	16 ft. broad	16 ft. broad	16 ft. broad	16 ft. broad
13 ft. broad	13 ft. broad	13 ft. broad	13 ft. broad	13 ft. broad
12 ft. broad	12 ft. broad	12 ft. broad	12 ft. broad	12 ft. broad
40 shot put	40 shot put	40 shot put	40 shot put	40 shot put
39 shot put	39 shot put	39 shot put	39 shot put	39 shot put
37 shot put	37 shot put	37 shot put	37 shot put	37 shot put
35 shot put	35 shot put	35 shot put	35 shot pu	35 shot put
30 shot put	30 shot put	30 shot put	30 shot put	30 shot put
16 ft. vault	16 ft. vault	16 ft. vault	16 ft. vault	16 ft. vault
15 ft. vault	15 ft. vault	15 ft. vault	15 ft. vault	15 ft. vault
14 ft. vault	14 ft. vault	14 ft. vault	14 ft. vault	14 ft. vault
13 ft. vault	13 ft. vault	13 ft. vault	13 ft. vault	13 ft. vault
12 ft. vault	12 ft. vault	12 ft. vault	12 ft. vault	12 ft. vault

12 And The Eat Goes On

THE STORY

Jack, Jane, Junior, Josie and Jim were very hungry. They went to an all-you-can-eat buffet restaurant determined to get their money's worth. They ate 22, 21, 20, 18 and 17 slices of pizza. They ate 32, 30, 28, 27 and 25 tacos. And they also ate 44, 42, 40, 38 and 34 fish sticks. Based on the clues, match the names with the number of pizza slices, tacos and fish sticks they ate.

THE CLUES

1. Jack, Jane and Junior each ate the most of one of the three food items.
2. Jack, Junior and Josie each ate the fewest of one of the three food items.
3. Jack and Jane ate a combined total of 35 slices of pizza, and Josie ate more pizza slices than Jim.
4. Jane ate more tacos than Jack, and Junior ate more fish sticks than Josie.
5. Junior ate exactly 2 more fish sticks than Jim, but Jane ate exactly 2 more fish sticks than Junior.
6. Jack ate exactly 2 more tacos than Josie.

Jack	Jane	Junior	Josie	Jim
22 pizza	22 pizza	22 pizza	22 pizza	22 pizza
21 pizza	21 pizza	21 pizza	21 pizza	21 pizza
20 pizza	20 pizza	20 pizza	20 pizza	20 pizza
18 pizza	18 pizza	18 pizza	18 pizza	18 pizza
17 pizza	17 pizza	17 pizza	17 pizza	17 pizza
32 tacos	32 tacos	32 tacos	32 tacos	32 tacos
30 tacos	30 tacos	30 tacos	30 tacos	30 tacos
28 tacos	28 tacos	28 tacos	28 tacos	28 tacos
27 tacos	27 tacos	27 tacos	27 tacos	27 tacos
25 tacos	25 tacos	25 tacos	25 tacos	25 tacos
44 fish	44 fish	44 fish	44 fish	44 fish
42 fish	42 fish	42 fish	42 fish	42 fish
40 fish	40 fish	40 fish	40 fish	40 fish
38 fish	38 fish	38 fish	38 fish	38 fish
34 fish	34 fish	34 fish	34 fish	34 fish

13 Used Car Sales

THE STORY

In the year 2005, five used car salesmen sold one car each. Their names were Sam, Sharon, Sheila, Stan and Sophie. The cars had been sitting around the used car lot for quite a while and they were happy to make the sales. The cars were made in 1949, 1950, 1953, 1955 and 1960, which made them pretty old at the time of their sale. The mileage on the odometers read 97,500, 95,000, 94,500, 93,500 and 92,000 miles. The engines in the cars sold that year had 450, 425, 400, 300 and 150 horsepower. Based on the clues, match the names with the years of the cars they sold, their mileage and horsepower.

THE CLUES

1. The combined age of the cars Sam and Sharon sold was 95 years, and the combined age of the cars Sheila and Stan sold was 111 years in the year they were sold.
2. The newest car had the highest mileage but the lowest horsepower.
3. Stan did not sell the oldest car, and Sharon did not sell the newest car.
4. Sophie's car had exactly 25 more horsepower than Stan's car, and Sheila's car had exactly 25 less horsepower than Stan's car.
5. The car with the highest horsepower had the lowest mileage.
6. Sheila's car had higher mileage than Stan's car but lower mileage than Sharon's car.

Sam	Sharon	Sheila	Stan	Sophie
1949	1949	1949	1949	1949
1950	1950	1950	1950	1950
1953	1953	1953	1953	1953
1955	1955	1955	1955	1955
1960	1960	1960	1960	1960
97,500 miles	97,500 miles	97,500 miles	97,500 miles	97,500 miles
95,000 miles	95,000 miles	95,000 miles	95,000 miles	95,000 miles
94,500 miles	94,500 miles	94,500 miles	94,500 miles	94,500 miles
93,500 miles	93,500 miles	93,500 miles	93,500 miles	93,500 miles
92,000 miles	92,000 miles	92,000 miles	92,000 miles	92,000 miles
450 HP	450 HP	450 HP	450 HP	450 HP
425 HP	425 HP	425 HP	425 HP	425 HP
400 HP	400 HP	400 HP	400 HP	400 HP
300 HP	300 HP	300 HP	300 HP	300 HP
150 HP	150 HP	150 HP	150 HP	150 HP

14 Pet Store Sales

THE STORY

Diane, Daisy, David, Dina and Darlene all owned pet stores. One recent day, they met at a convention for owners of pet stores and compared monthly sales. They had sold 1,200, 800, 700, 600 and 500 puppies. They had sold 1,200, 800, 700, 600 and 500 birds. They had sold 1,200, 800, 700, 600 and 500 hamsters. Based on the clues, match the owners with the number of puppies, birds and hamsters they sold that month.

THE CLUES

1. David, Dina and Darlene each sold the most of one of the three types of pets sold that month.
2. Daisy, David and Dina each sold the fewest of one of the three types of pets sold that month.
3. Diane and Daisy sold a combined total of 1,100 puppies.
4. Dina sold exactly 100 more puppies than Darlene, and Darlene, of course, did not sell the most birds.
5. Diane and Darlene sold a combined total of 2,000 hamsters, and Daisy sold more birds than Darlene but not as many as Diane that month.
6. David sold fewer hamsters than Daisy that month.

Diane	Daisy	David	Dina	Darlene
1,200 puppies	1,200 puppies	1,200 puppies	1,200 puppies	1,200 puppies
800 puppies	800 puppies	800 puppies	800 puppies	800 puppies
700 puppies	700 puppies	700 puppies	700 puppies	700 puppies
600 puppies	600 puppies	600 puppies	600 puppies	600 puppies
500 puppies	500 puppies	500 puppies	500 puppies	500 puppies
1,200 birds	1,200 birds	1,200 birds	1,200 birds	1,200 birds
800 birds	800 birds	800 birds	800 birds	800 birds
700 birds	700 birds	700 birds	700 birds	700 birds
600 birds	600 birds	600 birds	600 birds	600 birds
500 birds	500 birds	500 birds	500 birds	500 birds
1,200 hamsters	1,200 hamsters	1,200 hamsters	1,200 hamsters	1,200 hamsters
800 hamsters	800 hamsters	800 hamsters	800 hamsters	800 hamsters
700 hamsters	700 hamsters	700 hamsters	700 hamsters	700 hamsters
600 hamsters	600 hamsters	600 hamsters	600 hamsters	600 hamsters
500 hamsters	500 hamsters	500 hamsters	500 hamsters	500 hamsters

15 Flower Power

THE STORY

Ben, Betty, Byron, Belle and Beverly all had record-setting sales at their individual florist shops. One recent day, they sold 11,988, 11,964, 11,940, 11,520 and 11,400 roses. On that same day, they sold 9,600, 9,480, 9,240, 9,228 and 9,216 daisies. They also sold 7,200, 6,708, 6,696, 6,660 and 6,600 posies that day. Based on the clues, match the florists with the number of roses, daisies and posies they sold on that record-setting day.

THE CLUES

1. Ben, Betty and Byron each sold the most of one type of flower, and they each sold the fewest of another type of flower.
2. Betty and Beverly sold a combined total of 1,910 dozen roses, and Ben and Betty sold a combined total of 1,949 dozen roses.
3. Byron sold more roses than Belle.
4. Betty sold exactly 10 dozen more daisies than Ben, and Beverly sold more daisies than Belle.
5. Betty only sold 1 dozen more posies than Belle.

Ben	Betty	Byron	Belle	Beverly
11,988 roses	11,988 roses	11,988 roses	11,988 roses	11,988 roses
11,964 roses	11,964 roses	11,964 roses	11,964 roses	11,964 roses
11,940 roses	11,940 roses	11,940 roses	11,940 roses	11,940 roses
11,520 roses	11,520 roses	11,520 roses	11,520 roses	11,520 roses
11,400 roses	11,400 roses	11,400 roses	11,400 roses	11,400 roses
9,600 daisies	9,600 daisies	9,600 daisies	9,600 daisies	9,600 daisies
9,480 daisies	9,480 daisies	9,480 daisies	9,480 daisies	9,480 daisies
9,240 daisies	9,240 daisies	9,240 daisies	9,240 daisies	9,240 daisies
9,228 daisies	9,228 daisies	9,228 daisies	9,228 daisies	9,228 daisies
9,216 daisies	9,216 daisies	9,216 daisies	9,216 daisies	9,216 daisies
7,200 posies	7,200 posies	7,200 posies	7,200 posies	7,200 posies
6,708 posies	6,708 posies	6,708 posies	6,708 posies	6,708 posies
6,696 posies	6,696 posies	6,696 posies	6,696 posies	6,696 posies
6,660 posies	6,660 posies	6,660 posies	6,660 posies	6,660 posies
6,600 posies	6,600 posies	6,600 posies	6,600 posies	6,600 posies

16 Bowling Numbers

THE STORY

Bert, Bill, Betsy, Bonnie and Bella all had a curious time bowling. They all bowled three games and finished with identical scores of 600 points each. In comparing their scores for all the games they realized that, despite having identical final scores of 600, nobody had the same score as anybody else in any of the games. In the first game, they scored 300, 290, 285, 280 and 270 points. In the second game, they scored 195, 190, 180, 160 and 100 points. In the third game, they scored 200, 155, 150, 130 and 115 points. Based on the clues, match the bowlers with their scores in the first, second and third games all resulting in a total of 600 points.

THE CLUES

1. All five players had final scores of 600 after playing three games, but no player had the same score as any other player in any of the three games they played.
2. Betsy and Bonnie scored a combined total of 590 points in the first game.
3. In the first game, Bill scored higher than Bert, but Bert scored higher than Bella.
4. In the second game, Bill and Betsy scored a combined total of 260 points.
5. In the second game, Bonnie scored higher than Bert and Bella.
6. Bert scored 130 in the third game.
7. In the second game, Betsy scored lower than Bill.

Bert	Bill	Betsy	Bonnie	Bella
1st–300	1st–300	1st–300	1st–300	1st–300
1st–290	1st–290	1st–290	1st–290	1st–290
1st–285	1st–285	1st–285	1st–285	1st–285
1st–280	1st–280	1st–280	1st–280	1st–280
1st–270	1st–270	1st–270	1st–270	1st–270
2nd–195	2nd–195	2nd–195	2nd–195	2nd–195
2nd–190	2nd–190	2nd–190	2nd–190	2nd–190
2nd–180	2nd–180	2nd–180	2nd–180	2nd–180
2nd–160	2nd–160	2nd–160	2nd–160	2nd–160
2nd–100	2nd–100	2nd–100	2nd–100	2nd–100
3rd–200	3rd–200	3rd–200	3rd–200	3rd–200
3rd–155	3rd–155	3rd–155	3rd–155	3rd–155
3rd–150	3rd–150	3rd–150	3rd–150	3rd–150
3rd–130	3rd–130	3rd–130	3rd–130	3rd–130
3rd–1115	3rd–1115	3rd–1115	3rd–1115	3rd–1115

17 Acme Corporation

THE STORY

The Acme Corporation had five factories all making widgets and gizmos. The factories were named A, B, C, D and E. The factories made 10,000, 9,900, 9,600, 9,400 and 9,000 widgets. The factories made 2,000, 1,980, 1,800, 1,700 and 1,500 gizmos. Unfortunately, the factories occasionally had problems with quality control and had some defective widgets and gizmos returned to the factory. The factories combined the returned widgets and gizmos and kept a record of total returns. The total returns for the factories were 2,276, 2,160, 1,170, 1,160 and 1,140 returns. Based on the clues, match the factories with their production of widgets and gizmos and their total returns.

THE CLUES

1. Factory A made the most of one of the two manufactured items, and Factory E made the most of one of the two manufactured items.
2. Factory B made the fewest of one of the two manufactured items, and Factory D made the fewest of one of the two manufactured items.
3. Factory E produced exactly 600 more widgets than Factory C.
4. Factory D produced exactly 100 more gizmos than Factory E.
5. Factory B produced more widgets than Factory A.
6. The return rate on the total production of widgets and gizmos for Factory A, Factory B, and Factory E was 10%.
7. The return rate on the total production of widgets and gizmos for Factory C and for Factory D was 20%.

A	B	C	D	E
10,000 widgets	10,000 widgets	10,000 widgets	10,000 widgets	10,000 widgets
9,900 widgets	9,900 widgets	9,900 widgets	9,900 widgets	9,900 widgets
9,600 widgets	9,600 widgets	9,600 widgets	9,600 widgets	9,600 widgets
9,400 widgets	9,400 widgets	9,400 widgets	9,400 widgets	9,400 widgets
9,000 widgets	9,000 widgets	9,000 widgets	9,000 widgets	9,000 widgets
2,000 gizmos	2,000 gizmos	2,000 gizmos	2,000 gizmos	2,000 gizmos
1,980 gizmos	1,980 gizmos	1,980 gizmos	1,980 gizmos	1,980 gizmos
1,800 gizmos	1,800 gizmos	1,800 gizmos	1,800 gizmos	1,800 gizmos
1,700 gizmos	1,700 gizmos	1,700 gizmos	1,700 gizmos	1,700 gizmos
1,500 gizmos	1,500 gizmos	1,500 gizmos	1,500 gizmos	1,500 gizmos
2,276 returns	2,276 returns	2,276 returns	2,276 returns	2,276 returns
2,160 returns	2,160 returns	2,160 returns	2,160 returns	2,160 returns
1,170 returns	1,170 returns	1,170 returns	1,170 returns	1,170 returns
1,160 returns	1,160 returns	1,160 returns	1,160 returns	1,160 returns
1,140 returns	1,140 returns	1,140 returns	1,140 returns	1,140 returns

18 Elephant Diets

THE STORY

Five elephants named Jimbo, Larry, Terry, Barry and Barney decided to go on a diet. The elephants were 65, 60, 50, 45 and 30 years old. They weighed 2,580, 2,200, 2,150, 2,100 and 2,050 pounds. After dieting for 30 days they weighed themselves and discovered they had lost 420, 410, 258, 220 and 215 pounds. Based on the clues, match the elephants with their ages, weights and pounds lost.

THE CLUES

1. Multiply Larry's age by 70 to discover his weight.
2. Multiply Terry's age by 41 to determine his weight.
3. Divide Barney's weight by his age to obtain the answer 43.
4. Jimbo was not the oldest elephant, and the oldest elephant weighed more than Jimbo.
5. Larry and Terry each lost 20% of their original weight, and the other three elephants each lost half that percentage.

Jimbo	Larry	Terry	Barry	Barney
65 years old	65 years old	65 years old	65 years old	65 years old
60 years old	60 years old	60 years old	60 years old	60 years old
50 years old	50 years old	50 years old	50 years old	50 years old
45 years old	45 years old	45 years old	45 years old	45 years old
30 years old	30 years old	30 years old	30 years old	30 years old
2,580 weight	2,580 weight	2,580 weight	2,580 weight	2,580 weight
2,200 weight	2,200 weight	2,200 weight	2,200 weight	2,200 weight
2,150 weight	2,150 weight	2,150 weight	2,150 weight	2,150 weight
2,100 weight	2,100 weight	2,100 weight	2,100 weight	2,100 weight
2,050 weight	2,050 weight	2,050 weight	2,050 weight	2,050 weight
420 lost	420 lost	420 lost	420 lost	420 lost
410 lost	410 lost	410 lost	410 lost	410 lost
258 lost	258 lost	258 lost	258 lost	258 lost
220 lost	220 lost	220 lost	220 lost	220 lost
215 lost	215 lost	215 lost	215 lost	215 lost

19 Selling Farmers

THE STORY

Five farmers named Alice, Bret, Calvin, Doris and Ernie set up roadside stands near their farms to sell some of their produce. They all sold the same four vegetables, and on one recent day they sold 1,250, 1,200, 1,100, 1,090 and 1,050 ears of corn. They sold 900, 850, 845, 840 and 800 potatoes. They sold 1,500, 1,450, 1,425, 1,400 and 1,390 tomatoes. They also sold 925, 900, 875, 800 and 775 beets. Based on the clues, match the farmers with the number of different kinds of vegetables they sold that day.

THE CLUES

1. Bret, Calvin, Doris and Ernie each sold the most of one of the four vegetables at their farm stands, and Alice sold the fewest of two of the four types of vegetables sold.
2. Bret sold exactly 50 fewer ears of corn than Alice.
3. Ernie sold exactly 50 more ears of corn than Doris.
4. Ernie sold exactly 50 more tomatoes than Alice.
5. Bret sold exactly 50 fewer potatoes than Calvin, and Bret did not sell the most tomatoes.
6. Doris sold more potatoes than Ernie, and Bret did not sell the fewest tomatoes.
7. Doris sold more beets than Calvin but fewer than Ernie.

Alice	Bret	Calvin	Doris	Ernie
1,250 corn	1,250 corn	1,250 corn	1,250 corn	1,250 corn
1,200 corn	1,200 corn	1,200 corn	1,200 corn	1,200 corn
1,100 corn	1,100 corn	1,100 corn	1,100 corn	1,100 corn
1,090 corn	1,090 corn	1,090 corn	1,090 corn	1,090 corn
1,050 corn	1,050 corn	1,050 corn	1,050 corn	1,050 corn
900 potatoes	900 potatoes	900 potatoes	900 potatoes	900 potatoes
850 potatoes	850 potatoes	850 potatoes	850 potatoes	850 potatoes
845 potatoes	845 potatoes	845 potatoes	845 potatoes	845 potatoes
840 potatoes	840 potatoes	840 potatoes	840 potatoes	840 potatoes
800 potatoes	800 potatoes	800 potatoes	800 potatoes	800 potatoes
1,500 tomatoes	1,500 tomatoes	1,500 tomatoes	1,500 tomatoes	1,500 tomatoes
1,450 tomatoes	1,450 tomatoes	1,450 tomatoes	1,450 tomatoes	1,450 tomatoes
1,425 tomatoes	1,425 tomatoes	1,425 tomatoes	1,425 tomatoes	1,425 tomatoes
1,400 tomatoes	1,400 tomatoes	1,400 tomatoes	1,400 tomatoes	1,400 tomatoes
1,390 tomatoes	1,390 tomatoes	1,390 tomatoes	1,390 tomatoes	1,390 tomatoes
925 beets	925 beets	925 beets	925 beets	925 beets
900 beets	900 beets	900 beets	900 beets	900 beets
875 beets	875 beets	875 beets	875 beets	875 beets
800 beets	800 beets	800 beets	800 beets	800 beets
775 beets	775 beets	775 beets	775 beets	775 beets

20 Restless Monkeys

THE STORY

Five monkeys named Bingo, Gingo, Tinko, Dingo and Ringo decided to hold four contests. They enjoyed chewing bubble gum, so their first contest was to see who could blow the biggest bubble. They blew bubbles that were 14, 10, 9, 7 and 5 inches in diameter. Their next contest was to see who could climb a tree the fastest; they climbed the tree in 90, 80, 70, 60 and 58 seconds. Next, they held a banana-tossing contest and tossed bananas 90, 80, 75, 72 and 66 feet. Finally, they held a lemonade-drinking contest and they drank 16, 14, 12, 10 and 8 pints of lemonade in a minute. Based on the clues, match the monkeys with their bubble sizes, tree climbing times, banana distances and lemonade amounts.

THE CLUES

1. Bingo and Gingo each scored the best in one contest and the worst in another contest, but Dingo and Ringo also each scored the best in one contest and the worst in another contest.
2. The diameter of Dingo's bubble was the same as the radius of Gingo's bubble, and the radius of Bingo's bubble was the same as the diameter of Ringo's bubble.
3. Divide Gingo's tree-climbing time number by Tinko's bubble diameter and the answer is ten.
4. Divide Tinko's tree-climbing number by Dinko's bubble diameter and the answer is ten.
5. Ringo climbed the tree in less than a minute, and Bingo climbed the tree in more than a minute.
6. Bingo did not drink the most lemonade, and Tinko drank more lemonade than Gingo but less than Ringo.
7. Ringo tossed a banana farther than Tinko but not as far as Gingo.

Bingo	Gingo	Tinko	Dingo	Ringo
14 inches	14 inches	14 inches	14 inches	14 inches
10 inches	10 inches	10 inches	10 inches	10 inches
9 inches	9 inches	9 inches	9 inches	9 inches
7 inches	7 inches	7 inches	7 inches	7 inches
5 inches	5 inches	5 inches	5 inches	5 inches
90 seconds	90 seconds	90 seconds	90 seconds	90 seconds
80 seconds	80 seconds	80 seconds	80 seconds	80 seconds
70 seconds	70 seconds	70 seconds	70 seconds	70 seconds
60 seconds	60 seconds	60 seconds	60 seconds	60 seconds
58 seconds	58 seconds	58 seconds	58 seconds	58 seconds
90 feet	90 feet	90 feet	90 feet	90 feet
80 feet	80 feet	80 feet	80 feet	80 feet
75 feet	75 feet	75 feet	75 feet	75 feet
72 feet	72 feet	72 feet	72 feet	72 feet
66 feet	66 feet	66 feet	66 feet	66 feet
16 pints	16 pints	16 pints	16 pints	16 pints
14 pints	14 pints	14 pints	14 pints	14 pints
12 pints	12 pints	12 pints	12 pints	12 pints
10 pints	10 pints	10 pints	10 pints	10 pints
8 pints	8 pints	8 pints	8 pints	8 pints

21 What's Up Dock?

THE STORY

Five sailors named Salty, Nemo, Windy, Kirk and Cookie each owned a sailing boat. The boats were 70, 50, 45, 40 and 29 feet in length. They had main masts that were 80, 70, 60, 55 and 50 feet tall. The longest voyages the sailors had been on were 10,000, 9,998, 9,500, 9,450 and 9,000 miles. These voyages had taken 90, 85, 80, 70 and 65 days to complete. Based on the clues, match the sailors with their boat lengths, their mast heights, the number of miles of their longest trips, and the days at sea to complete these trips.

THE CLUES

1. If you combined the length of Salty's boat with the length of Nemo's boat, the answer would be 40 yards, and if you combined the length of Kirk's boat with Cookie's boat, the answer would be 23 yards.
2. The combined height of Salty's mast and Nemo's mast was 35 yards, and the combined height of Kirk's mast and Cookie's mast was 50 yards.
3. Windy traveled exactly 500 miles less than Salty and exactly 500 miles more than Cookie and, of course Windy did not spend the most days at sea.
4. The longest boat spent the fewest days at sea, the boat with the tallest mast traveled the shortest distance in miles, and Nemo did not have the shortest mast.
5. One boat had a mast that had the same number in height of its mast as its length.
6. The sailor in the shortest boat went on a voyage that lasted exactly 20 more days than the sailor in the longest boat's voyage lasted.
7. Windy's voyage lasted longer than Salty's voyage, Kirk's boat was half as long as Cookie's mast, and Nemo sailed more miles than Kirk.

Salty	Nemo	Windy	Kirk	Cookie
70 ft. long	70 ft. long	70 ft. long	70 ft. long	70 ft. long
50 ft. long	50 ft. long	50 ft. long	50 ft. long	50 ft. long
45 ft. long	45 ft. long	45 ft. long	45 ft. long	45 ft. long
40 ft. long	40 ft. long	40 ft. long	40 ft. long	40 ft. long
29 ft. long	29 ft. long	29 ft. long	29 ft. long	29 ft. long
80 ft. mast	80 ft. mast	80 ft. mast	80 ft. mast	80 ft. mast
70 ft. mast	70 ft. mast	70 ft. mast	70 ft. mast	70 ft. mast
60 ft. mast	60 ft. mast	60 ft. mast	60 ft. mast	60 ft. mast
55 ft. mast	55 ft. mast	55 ft. mast	55 ft. mast	55 ft. mast
50 ft. mast	50 ft. mast	50 ft. mast	50 ft. mast	50 ft. mast
10,000 miles	10,000 miles	10,000 miles	10,000 miles	10,000 miles
9,998 miles	9,998 miles	9,998 miles	9,998 miles	9,998 miles
9,500 miles	9,500 miles	9,500 miles	9,500 miles	9,500 miles
9,450 miles	9,450 miles	9,450 miles	9,450 miles	9,450 miles
9,000 miles	9,000 miles	9,000 miles	9,000 miles	9,000 miles
90 days	90 days	90 days	90 days	90 days
85 days	85 days	85 days	85 days	85 days
80 days	80 days	80 days	80 days	80 days
70 days	70 days	70 days	70 days	70 days
65 days	65 days	65 days	65 days	65 days

22 Wood You Be Mine?

THE STORY

Willie, Wilma, Walt, Wallis and Waylon were five carpenters who were hired to build wooden rectangular shaped decks. The decks were 30, 28, 25, 21 and 20 feet in length and 10, 9, 8, 7 and 5 feet in width. The carpenters used 400, 390, 370, 350 and 300 nails in constructing the decks. The cost for building the decks was $5,000, $4,500, $4,250, $4,100 and $4,000. Based on the clues, match the carpenters with the lengths, widths, nails and costs.

THE CLUES

1. Willie and Wilma each built decks that were exactly 210 square feet, they used a combined total of 790 nails, and the combined cost of the two decks was $8,100.
2. Waylon's deck was exactly 100 square feet and was not the most expensive deck, but it did cost more than Walt's deck.
3. Walt's deck was exactly 52 square feet bigger than Wallis' deck.
4. The smallest deck used the fewest nails, and the least expensive deck used the most nails.
5. Willie's deck had the greatest width, and Wilma and Wallis used a combined total of 740 nails.

Willie	Wilma	Walt	Wallis	Waylon
30 ft. length	30 ft. length	30 ft. length	30 ft. length	30 ft. length
28 ft. length	28 ft. length	28 ft. length	28 ft. length	28 ft. length
25 ft. length	25 ft. length	25 ft. length	25 ft. length	25 ft. length
21 ft. length	21 ft. length	21 ft. length	21 ft. length	21 ft. length
20 ft. length	20 ft. length	20 ft. length	20 ft. length	20 ft. length
10 ft. width	10 ft. width	10 ft. width	10 ft. width	10 ft. width
9 ft. width	9 ft. width	9 ft. width	9 ft. width	9 ft. width
8 ft. width	8 ft. width	8 ft. width	8 ft. width	8 ft. width
7 ft. width	7 ft. width	7 ft. width	7 ft. width	7 ft. width
5 ft. width	5 ft. width	5 ft. width	5 ft. width	5 ft. width
400 nails	400 nails	400 nails	400 nails	400 nails
390 nails	390 nails	390 nails	390 nails	390 nails
370 nails	370 nails	370 nails	370 nails	370 nails
350 nails	350 nails	350 nails	350 nails	350 nails
300 nails	300 nails	300 nails	300 nails	300 nails
$5,000	$5,000	$5,000	$5,000	$5,000
$4,500	$4,500	$4,500	$4,500	$4,500
$4,250	$4,250	$4,250	$4,250	$4,250
$4,100	$4,100	$4,100	$4,100	$4,100
$4,000	$4,000	$4,000	$4,000	$4,000

23 Just Pottering Around

THE STORY

Peter, Patty, Penny, Paul and Pierre were five potters living and working in the town of Peeterville. One recent day, they decided to compete against each other in a series of contests. The first three contests were to see who could make the most cups, saucers and vases in an eight-hour day. The fourth contest was to see who could make a plate with the largest diameter. They made 90, 85, 80, 70 and 65 cups. They made 140, 130, 120, 110 and 100 saucers. And they made 70, 65, 60, 50 and 45 vases. Finally, they made plates that were 50, 40, 30, 25 and 20 inches in diameter. Based on the clues, match the potters with the number of cups, saucers and vases they made, and the diameter of the plates they made.

THE CLUES

1. The radius of Patty's plate was the same as the diameter of Paul's plate, and the diameter of Pierre's plate was the same as the radius of Peter's plate.
2. Peter made the most of one item, Patty made the most of another item, and Penny made the most of yet another item.
3. Peter and Penny made a combined total of 170 cups, and Pierre made exactly 5 more cups than Paul.
4. Penny and Paul made a combined total of 270 saucers while Peter and Penny made a combined total of 240 saucers.
5. Pierre's plate was bigger than Paul's plate, and Paul's vase number was exactly one-half the size of Peter's saucer number.
6. Penny made more vases than Pierre but fewer than Peter, and Pierre made exactly 10 more saucers than Patty.

Peter	Patty	Penny	Paul	Pierre
90 cups	90 cups	90 cups	90 cups	90 cups
85 cups	85 cups	85 cups	85 cups	85 cups
80 cups	80 cups	80 cups	80 cups	80 cups
70 cups	70 cups	70 cups	70 cups	70 cups
65 cups	65 cups	65 cups	65 cups	65 cups
140 saucers	140 saucers	140 saucers	140 saucers	140 saucers
130 saucers	130 saucers	130 saucers	130 saucers	130 saucers
120 saucers	120 saucers	120 saucers	120 saucers	120 saucers
110 saucers	110 saucers	110 saucers	110 saucers	110 saucers
100 saucers	100 saucers	100 saucers	100 saucers	100 saucers
70 vases	70 vases	70 vases	70 vases	70 vases
65 vases	65 vases	65 vases	65 vases	65 vases
60 vases	60 vases	60 vases	60 vases	60 vases
50 vases	50 vases	50 vases	50 vases	50 vases
45 vases	45 vases	45 vases	45 vases	45 vases
50 inches	50 inches	50 inches	50 inches	50 inches
40 inches	40 inches	40 inches	40 inches	40 inches
30 inches	30 inches	30 inches	30 inches	30 inches
25 inches	25 inches	25 inches	25 inches	25 inches
20 inches	20 inches	20 inches	20 inches	20 inches

24 A Classy Picnic

THE STORY

Donna, Drake, Debra, Diane and David were five teachers at the Pleasant Ridge School. They had 20, 18, 17, 15 and 12 boys in their classrooms. They had 19, 16, 14, 13 and 11 girls in their classrooms. One recent day, they took their classes on a picnic. At the picnic, their classes ate 100, 95, 90, 80 and 70 hot dogs. Their classes drank 200, 180, 160, 140 and 100 glasses of lemonade. Based on the clues, match the teachers with the number of boys and girls in their classrooms, and the number of hot dogs their classes ate, and glasses of lemonade their classes drank.

THE CLUES

1. Diane had the highest numbers in two of the four categories, and David had the highest numbers in two of the four categories.
2. Donna had the lowest numbers in two of the four categories, and Drake had the lowest numbers in two of the four categories.
3. Donna and Drake's combined total of boys was 27, and Diane and David's combined total of boys was 38.
4. David's class had more girls than boys, Donna and Drake's combined total of girls was 24, and David's class ate exactly 10 more hot dogs than Donna's class but exactly 10 less than Drake's class.
5. Donna had more girls than boys in her class, and Diane had more girls than Debra in her class.
6. Multiply Diane's number of girls by 10 to find Debra's lemonade number, and multiply Debra's number of girls by 10 to determine Diane's lemonade number.

Donna	Drake	Debra	Diane	David
20 boys	20 boys	20 boys	20 boys	20 boys
18 boys	18 boys	18 boys	18 boys	18 boys
17 boys	17 boys	17 boys	17 boys	17 boys
15 boys	15 boys	15 boys	15 boys	15 boys
12 boys	12 boys	12 boys	12 boys	12 boys
19 girls	19 girls	19 girls	19 girls	19 girls
16 girls	16 girls	16 girls	16 girls	16 girls
14 girls	14 girls	14 girls	14 girls	14 girls
13 girls	13 girls	13 girls	13 girls	13 girls
11 girls	11 girls	11 girls	11 girls	11 girls
100 hot dogs	100 hot dogs	100 hot dogs	100 hot dogs	100 hot dogs
95 hot dogs	95 hot dogs	95 hot dogs	95 hot dogs	95 hot dogs
90 hot dogs	90 hot dogs	90 hot dogs	90 hot dogs	90 hot dogs
80 hot dogs	80 hot dogs	80 hot dogs	80 hot dogs	80 hot dogs
70 hot dogs	70 hot dogs	70 hot dogs	70 hot dogs	70 hot dogs
200 glasses	200 glasses	200 glasses	200 glasses	200 glasses
180 glasses	180 glasses	180 glasses	180 glasses	180 glasses
160 glasses	160 glasses	160 glasses	160 glasses	160 glasses
140 glasses	140 glasses	140 glasses	140 glasses	140 glasses
100 glasses	100 glasses	100 glasses	100 glasses	100 glasses

25 Squat's Happening?

THE STORY

Eddie, Edris, Ellie, Eliot and Ernie all belonged to the same exercise class. One recent day, they decided to hold four contests to see who could do the most push-ups, sit-ups, pull-ups, and squats in an hour. They did 550, 525, 500, 490 and 480 push-ups. They did 1,100, 1,050, 1,000, 980 and 900 sit-ups. They did 150, 125, 100, 90 and 70 pull-ups. They did 300, 295, 290, 280 and 270 squats. Based on the clues, match the names with the number of push-ups, sit-ups, pull-ups and squats they performed in the contests.

THE CLUES

1. Eddie, Edris, Ellie and Eliot each did the most of one of the four exercises but each also did the fewest of one of the four exercises.
2. Eddie and Edris' combined push-up total was 970 push-ups, and Ellie and Eliot's combined push-up total was 1,075 push-ups.
3. Multiply Ernie's push-up total by 2 to reveal Edris' sit-up total.
4. Edris did not do the most squats but she did exactly 10 more squats than Eddie.
5. Ellie did more push-ups than Eliot, Ellie did more pull-ups than Eliot and Ernie, and she even did exactly 10 more squats than Edris.
6. Eddie did more pull-ups than Ernie and Ellie, and Eliot did more sit-ups than Ernie.

Eddie	Edris	Ellie	Eliot	Ernie
550 push-ups	550 push-ups	550 push-ups	550 push-ups	550 push-ups
525 push-ups	525 push-ups	525 push-ups	525 push-ups	525 push-ups
500 push-ups	500 push-ups	500 push-ups	500 push-ups	500 push-ups
490 push-ups	490 push-ups	490 push-ups	490 push-ups	490 push-ups
480 push-ups	480 push-ups	480 push-ups	480 push-ups	480 push-ups
1,100 sit-ups	1,100 sit-ups	1,100 sit-ups	1,100 sit-ups	1,100 sit-ups
1,050 sit-ups	1,050 sit-ups	1,050 sit-ups	1,050 sit-ups	1,050 sit-ups
1,000 sit-ups	1,000 sit-ups	1,000 sit-ups	1,000 sit-ups	1,000 sit-ups
980 sit-ups	980 sit-ups	980 sit-ups	980 sit-ups	980 sit-ups
900 sit-ups	900 sit-ups	900 sit-ups	900 sit-ups	900 sit-ups
150 pull-ups	150 pull-ups	150 pull-ups	150 pull-ups	150 pull-ups
125 pull-ups	125 pull-ups	125 pull-ups	125 pull-ups	125 pull-ups
100 pull-ups	100 pull-ups	100 pull-ups	100 pull-ups	100 pull-ups
90 pull-ups	90 pull-ups	90 pull-ups	90 pull-ups	90 pull-ups
70 pull-ups	70 pull-ups	70 pull-ups	70 pull-ups	70 pull-ups
300 squats	300 squats	300 squats	300 squats	300 squats
295 squats	295 squats	295 squats	295 squats	295 squats
290 squats	290 squats	290 squats	290 squats	290 squats
280 squats	280 squats	280 squats	280 squats	280 squats
270 squats	270 squats	270 squats	270 squats	270 squats

26 I Herd That

THE STORY

The towns of Alpha, Beta, Crown, Dofuss and Enid kept herds of different kinds of animals. They all kept herds of elk, bison, reindeer and antelope. They had 1,000, 800, 500, 400 and 300 elk. They had 1,000, 800, 500, 400 and 300 bison. They had 1,000, 800, 500, 400 and 300 reindeer. They had 1,000, 800, 500, 400 and 300 antelope. Based on the clues, match the towns with the sizes of their elk, bison, reindeer and antelope herds.

THE CLUES

1. No town had the same number of animals in one herd as it had in another herd. If a town had 1,000 elk it did not have 1,000 of anything else, and so on.
2. Crown had twice as many elk as Enid, and Beta had half as many elk as Dofuss.
3. Crown had twice as many bison as Alpha, and Dofuss had half as many bison as Enid.
4. Crown had half as many reindeer as Alpha, and Beta had twice as many reindeer as Dofuss.
5. Beta had twice as many antelope as Alpha, and Crown had half as many antelope as Enid.
6. Crown had more elk than Dofuss.

Alpha	Beta	Crown	Dofuss	Enid
1,000 elk	1,000 elk	1,000 elk	1,000 elk	1,000 elk
800 elk	800 elk	800 elk	800 elk	800 elk
500 elk	500 elk	500 elk	500 elk	500 elk
400 elk	400 elk	400 elk	400 elk	400 elk
300 elk	300 elk	300 elk	300 elk	300 elk
1,000 bison	1,000 bison	1,000 bison	1,000 bison	1,000 bison
800 bison	800 bison	800 bison	800 bison	800 bison
500 bison	500 bison	500 bison	500 bison	500 bison
400 bison	400 bison	400 bison	400 bison	400 bison
300 bison	300 bison	300 bison	300 bison	300 bison
1,000 reindeer	1,000 reindeer	1,000 reindeer	1,000 reindeer	1,000 reindeer
800 reindeer	800 reindeer	800 reindeer	800 reindeer	800 reindeer
500 reindeer	500 reindeer	500 reindeer	500 reindeer	500 reindeer
400 reindeer	400 reindeer	400 reindeer	400 reindeer	400 reindeer
300 reindeer	300 reindeer	300 reindeer	300 reindeer	300 reindeer
1,000 antelope	1,000 antelope	1,000 antelope	1,000 antelope	1,000 antelope
800 antelope	800 antelope	800 antelope	800 antelope	800 antelope
500 antelope	500 antelope	500 antelope	500 antelope	500 antelope
400 antelope	400 antelope	400 antelope	400 antelope	400 antelope
300 antelope	300 antelope	300 antelope	300 antelope	300 antelope

27 Amusement Parking

THE STORY

Chet, Carla, Carol, Champ and Celine loved to visit amusement parks. They had visited 225, 215, 205, 185 and 170 different amusement parks in their lives. At the parks, they had ridden 1,000, 900, 800, 750 and 700 different roller coasters. They had ridden 400, 375, 350, 300 and 200 different Ferris wheels. They had taken rides on 2,500, 2,250, 2,000, 1,250 and 1,000 different merry-go-rounds. Based on the clues, match the names with the number of parks they visited, and the number of roller coasters, Ferris wheels and merry-go-rounds they had ridden.

THE CLUES

1. Chet and Carla visited a combined total of 355 parks, and Champ and Celine visited a combined total of 440 parks.
2. Chet took a combined total of 3,900 rides on roller coasters, Ferris wheels, and merry-go-rounds.
3. Celine took a combined total of 1,900 rides on roller coasters, Ferris wheels, and merry-go-rounds.
4. Multiply Carol's Ferris wheel number by 2 to discover Celine's roller coaster number.
5. Multiply Chet's Ferris wheel number by 2 to reveal Carol's roller coaster number.
6. The person who took the most total rides visited the fewest parks, and the person who took the fewest total rides visited the most parks.
7. Carol took exactly 250 fewer merry-go-round rides than Carla.
8. Champ took more Ferris wheel rides than Carla, and Carla took more roller coaster rides than Champ.

Chet	Carla	Carol	Champ	Celine
225 parks	225 parks	225 parks	225 parks	225 parks
215 parks	215 parks	215 parks	215 parks	215 parks
205 parks	205 parks	205 parks	205 parks	205 parks
185 parks	185 parks	185 parks	185 parks	185 parks
170 parks	170 parks	170 parks	170 parks	170 parks
1,000 roller	1,000 roller	1,000 roller	1,000 roller	1,000 roller
900 roller	900 roller	900 roller	900 roller	900 roller
800 roller	800 roller	800 roller	800 roller	800 roller
750 roller	750 roller	750 roller	750 roller	750 roller
700 roller	700 roller	700 roller	700 roller	700 roller
400 Ferris	400 Ferris	400 Ferris	400 Ferris	400 Ferris
375 Ferris	375 Ferris	375 Ferris	375 Ferris	375 Ferris
350 Ferris	350 Ferris	350 Ferris	350 Ferris	350 Ferris
300 Ferris	300 Ferris	300 Ferris	300 Ferris	300 Ferris
200 Ferris	200 Ferris	200 Ferris	200 Ferris	200 Ferris
2,500 m-g-r	2,500 m-g-r	2,500 m-g-r	2,500 m-g-r	2,500 m-g-r
2,250 m-g-r	2,250 m-g-r	2,250 m-g-r	2,250 m-g-r	2,250 m-g-r
2,000 m-g-r	2,000 m-g-r	2,000 m-g-r	2,000 m-g-r	2,000 m-g-r
1,250 m-g-r	1,250 m-g-r	1,250 m-g-r	1,250 m-g-r	1,250 m-g-r
1,000 m-g-r	1,000 m-g-r	1,000 m-g-r	1,000 m-g-r	1,000 m-g-r

 |

28 Something Fishy

THE STORY

Five people named Victor, Vinnie, Val, Vera and Violet owned fishing boats. One recent day, they decided to have a contest to see who could catch the most of the four types of seafood they usually tried to catch. They caught 1,500, 1,450, 1,400, 1,300 and 1,000 pounds of shrimp. They caught 750, 725, 700, 600 and 500 pounds of perch. They caught 3,000, 2,900, 2,800, 2,000 and 1,500 pounds of tuna. They caught 400, 350, 300, 200 and 100 pounds of flounder. Based on the clues, match the names with the pounds of shrimp, perch, tuna and flounder they caught on the day of the contest.

THE CLUES

1. Victor caught the most of two types of seafood, and Vinnie caught the most of two types of seafood.
2. Victor caught the least of two types of seafood, and Vinnie caught the least of two types of seafood.
3. Val caught twice as much flounder as Vinnie.
4. Multiply Vera's flounder number by 10 to find Vinnie's tuna number, and Vinnie and Val's combined shrimp total was 2,950.
5. Vera's perch number was half the size of her shrimp number, and Val's flounder number was one-third her perch number.
6. Victor and Vera's combined tuna number was 3,500 and, of course, Violet caught more tuna than Val.

Victor	Vinnie	Val	Vera	Violet
1,500 shrimp	1,500 shrimp	1,500 shrimp	1,500 shrimp	1,500 shrimp
1,450 shrimp	1,450 shrimp	1,450 shrimp	1,450 shrimp	1,450 shrimp
1,400 shrimp	1,400 shrimp	1,400 shrimp	1,400 shrimp	1,400 shrimp
1,300 shrimp	1,300 shrimp	1,300 shrimp	1,300 shrimp	1,300 shrimp
1,000 shrimp	1,000 shrimp	1,000 shrimp	1,000 shrimp	1,000 shrimp
750 perch	750 perch	750 perch	750 perch	750 perch
725 perch	725 perch	725 perch	725 perch	725 perch
700 perch	700 perch	700 perch	700 perch	700 perch
600 perch	600 perch	600 perch	600 perch	600 perch
500 perch	500 perch	500 perch	500 perch	500 perch
3,000 tuna	3,000 tuna	3,000 tuna	3,000 tuna	3,000 tuna
2,900 tuna	2,900 tuna	2,900 tuna	2,900 tuna	2,900 tuna
2,800 tuna	2,800 tuna	2,800 tuna	2,800 tuna	2,800 tuna
2,000 tuna	2,000 tuna	2,000 tuna	2,000 tuna	2,000 tuna
1,500 tuna	1,500 tuna	1,500 tuna	1,500 tuna	1,500 tuna
400 flounder	400 flounder	400 flounder	400 flounder	400 flounder
350 flounder	350 flounder	350 flounder	350 flounder	350 flounder
300 flounder	300 flounder	300 flounder	300 flounder	300 flounder
200 flounder	200 flounder	200 flounder	200 flounder	200 flounder
100 flounder	100 flounder	100 flounder	100 flounder	100 flounder

29 Quadruple Play

THE STORY

Alvin, Alice, Arthur, Annie and Albert recently took trips to four different countries. They spent 12, 10, 9, 8 and 7 days in France. They spent 12, 10, 9, 8 and 7 days in England. They spent 12, 10, 9, 8 and 7 days in Spain. They spent 12, 10, 9, 8 and 7 days in Italy. Based on the clues, match the names with the days they each spent in France, England, Spain and Italy.

THE CLUES

1. Arthur spent a total of 36 days visiting the four countries and he was the only one to spend the same amount of time in more than one country and, of course, he always spent more than 8 days in each country.
2. Alvin, Alice, Annie and Albert each spent 37 days visiting other countries.
3. Alvin and Alice spent a combined total of 15 days in France and 15 days in Spain.
4. Alice and Annie spent a combined total of 18 days in France.
5. Alvin and Albert spent a combined total of 17 days in England.

Alvin	Alice	Arthur	Annie	Albert
12 France	12 France	12 France	12 France	12 France
10 France	10 France	10 France	10 France	10 France
9 France	9 France	9 France	9 France	9 France
8 France	8 France	8 France	8 France	8 France
7 France	7 France	7 France	7 France	7 France
12 England	12 England	12 England	12 England	12 England
10 England	10 England	10 England	10 England	10 England
9 England	9 England	9 England	9 England	9 England
8 England	8 England	8 England	8 England	8 England
7 England	7 England	7 England	7 England	7 England
12 Spain	12 Spain	12 Spain	12 Spain	12 Spain
10 Spain	10 Spain	10 Spain	10 Spain	10 Spain
9 Spain	9 Spain	9 Spain	9 Spain	9 Spain
8 Spain	8 Spain	8 Spain	8 Spain	8 Spain
7 Spain	7 Spain	7 Spain	7 Spain	7 Spain
12 Italy	12 Italy	12 Italy	12 Italy	12 Italy
10 Italy	10 Italy	10 Italy	10 Italy	10 Italy
9 Italy	9 Italy	9 Italy	9 Italy	9 Italy
8 Italy	8 Italy	8 Italy	8 Italy	8 Italy
7 Italy	7 Italy	7 Italy	7 Italy	7 Italy

30 Bling It On

THE STORY

Pierre, Pamela, Patrick, Paula and Peter all owned jewelry stores. At a jewelers convention they compared monthly sales of their four most popular items. They sold 450, 425, 400, 350 and 300 watches. They sold 500, 475, 460, 440 and 420 pairs of earrings. They sold 1,000, 900, 850, 800 and 700 rings. They sold 100, 90, 75, 70 and 50 necklaces. Based on the clues, match the jewelers with the number of watches, pairs of earrings, rings and necklaces they sold.

THE CLUES

1. Pierre, Pamela, Patrick and Paula each sold the most of one item and they each also sold the fewest of one item.
2. Paula and Peter sold a combined total of 140 necklaces, and Paula and Peter sold a combined total of 875 watches.
3. Patrick and Peter sold a combined total of 975 pairs of earrings, and Patrick sold exactly 50 more watches than Pierre.
4. Pamela sold exactly 20 more pairs of earrings than Paula.
5. Multiply Pierre's necklace number by 10 to identify Pamela's ring number.
6. Divide Patrick's ring number by 10 to determine Pamela's necklace number.
7. Pierre sold more rings than Paula, but Peter sold more rings than Pierre.

Pierre	Pamela	Patrick	Paula	Peter
450 watches	450 watches	450 watches	450 watches	450 watches
425 watches	425 watches	425 watches	425 watches	425 watches
400 watches	400 watches	400 watches	400 watches	400 watches
350 watches	350 watches	350 watches	350 watches	350 watches
300 watches	300 watches	300 watches	300 watches	300 watches
500 earrings	500 earrings	500 earrings	500 earrings	500 earrings
475 earrings	475 earrings	475 earrings	475 earrings	475 earrings
460 earrings	460 earrings	460 earrings	460 earrings	460 earrings
440 earrings	440 earrings	440 earrings	440 earrings	440 earrings
420 earrings	420 earrings	420 earrings	420 earrings	420 earrings
1,000 rings	1,000 rings	1,000 rings	1,000 rings	1,000 rings
900 rings	900 rings	900 rings	900 rings	900 rings
850 rings	850 rings	850 rings	850 rings	850 rings
800 rings	800 rings	800 rings	800 rings	800 rings
700 rings	700 rings	700 rings	700 rings	700 rings
100 necklaces	100 necklaces	100 necklaces	100 necklaces	100 necklaces
90 necklaces	90 necklaces	90 necklaces	90 necklaces	90 necklaces
75 necklaces	75 necklaces	75 necklaces	75 necklaces	75 necklaces
70 necklaces	70 necklaces	70 necklaces	70 necklaces	70 necklaces
50 necklaces	50 necklaces	50 necklaces	50 necklaces	50 necklaces

31 It's A Hit!

THE STORY

Five Internet bloggers named Randy, Raul, Rita, Rick and Ruth recently got together and compared the number of hits their blogs had received in the months of April, May, June and July. In April, they received 10,000, 9,950, 9,750, 9,700 and 9,500 hits. In May, they received 20,000, 19,900, 19,500, 19,400 and 19,000 hits. In June, they received 40,000, 39,800, 19,500, 19,000 and 15,000 hits. In July, they received 80,000, 79,600, 38,000, 34,000 and 30,000 hits. Based on the clues, match the bloggers with the number of hits they received in April, May, June and July.

THE CLUES

1. Randy had the most hits in two of the months, and Raul had the most hits in two of the months.
2. Rick had the fewest hits in two of the months, and Ruth had the fewest hits in two of the months.
3. Rita was always in the top three for all four months, but Randy and Raul were also in the top three for all four months.
4. Multiply Raul's April hits by 4 to find the number of June hits he got.
5. In April and June Ruth had more hits than Rick, and in May Rita had exactly 400 more hits than Raul.
6. In June, Randy had more hits than Rita but fewer than Raul, and in July, Rita had exactly 4,000 more hits than Rick.
7. Rita had more hits than Randy in only one of the four months.

Randy	Raul	Rita	Rick	Ruth
April 10,000	April 10,000	April 10,000	April 10,000	April 10,000
April 9,950	April 9,950	April 9,950	April 9,950	April 9,950
April 9,750	April 9,750	April 9,750	April 9,750	April 9,750
April 9,700	April 9,700	April 9,700	April 9,700	April 9,700
April 9,500	April 9,500	April 9,500	April 9,500	April 9,500
May 20,000	May 20,000	May 20,000	May 20,000	May 20,000
May 19,900	May 19,900	May 19,900	May 19,900	May 19,900
May 19,500	May 19,500	May 19,500	May 19,500	May 19,500
May 19,400	May 19,400	May 19,400	May 19,400	May 19,400
May 19,000	May 19,000	May 19,000	May 19,000	May 19,000
June 40,000	June 40,000	June 40,000	June 40,000	June 40,000
June 39,800	June 39,800	June 39,800	June 39,800	June 39,800
June 19,500	June 19,500	June 19,500	June 19,500	June 19,500
June 19,000	June 19,000	June 19,000	June 19,000	June 19,000
June 15,000	June 15,000	June 15,000	June 15,000	June 15,000
July 80,000	July 80,000	July 80,000	July 80,000	July 80,000
July 79,600	July 79,600	July 79,600	July 79,600	July 79,600
July 38,000	July 38,000	July 38,000	July 38,000	July 38,000
July 34,000	July 34,000	July 34,000	July 34,000	July 34,000
July 30,000	July 30,000	July 30,000	July 30,000	July 30,000

32 Save A Coin

THE STORY

Zack, Zelda, Zoe, Zoltan and Zorba loved to save coins and they saved a lot of them. They only collected quarters, dimes, nickels and pennies. They saved 2,200, 2,100, 2,000, 1,700 and 1,200 quarters. They saved 14,000, 13,500, 13,000, 12,000 and 10,000 dimes. They saved 25,000, 23,000, 22,500, 21,000 and 19,000 nickels. They saved 50,000, 46,000, 45,000, 42,000 and 38,000 pennies. Based on the clues, match the names with the number of quarters, dimes, nickels and pennies they had saved.

THE CLUES

1. Zack and Zelda had a combined total of $725 worth of quarters, and Zoltan and Zorba had a combined total of $1,075 worth of quarters.
2. Zoltan and Zorba had a combined total of $2,750 worth of dimes, and Zack and Zelda had a combined total of $2,200 worth of dimes.
3. Zack and Zelda had a combined total of $2,000 worth of nickels, and Zoltan and Zorba had a combined total of $2,400 worth of nickels.
4. Zoltan and Zorba had a combined total of $960 worth of pennies, and Zack and Zelda had a combined total of $800 worth of pennies.
5. Zack's coins were worth a total of $2,855, and Zoltan's coins were worth a total of $3,610.
6. Zack had more quarters than Zelda, Zoltan had more quarters than Zorba, Zelda had more dimes than Zack, and Zorba had more dimes than Zoltan.

Zack	Zelda	Zoe	Zoltan	Zorba
2,200 quarters	2,200 quarters	2,200 quarters	2,200 quarters	2,200 quarters
2,100 quarters	2,100 quarters	2,100 quarters	2,100 quarters	2,100 quarters
2,000 quarters	2,000 quarters	2,000 quarters	2,000 quarters	2,000 quarters
1,700 quarters	1,700 quarters	1,700 quarters	1,700 quarters	1,700 quarters
1,200 quarters	1,200 quarters	1,200 quarters	1,200 quarters	1,200 quarters
14,000 dimes	14,000 dimes	14,000 dimes	14,000 dimes	14,000 dimes
13,500 dimes	13,500 dimes	13,500 dimes	13,500 dimes	13,500 dimes
13,000 dimes	13,000 dimes	13,000 dimes	13,000 dimes	13,000 dimes
12,000 dimes	12,000 dimes	12,000 dimes	12,000 dimes	12,000 dimes
10,000 dimes	10,000 dimes	10,000 dimes	10,000 dimes	10,000 dimes
25,000 nickels	25,000 nickels	25,000 nickels	25,000 nickels	25,000 nickels
23,000 nickels	23,000 nickels	23,000 nickels	23,000 nickels	23,000 nickels
22,500 nickels	22,500 nickels	22,500 nickels	22,500 nickels	22,500 nickels
21,000 nickels	21,000 nickels	21,000 nickels	21,000 nickels	21,000 nickels
19,000 nickels	19,000 nickels	19,000 nickels	19,000 nickels	19,000 nickels
50,000 pennies	50,000 pennies	50,000 pennies	50,000 pennies	50,000 pennies
46,000 pennies	46,000 pennies	46,000 pennies	46,000 pennies	46,000 pennies
45,000 pennies	45,000 pennies	45,000 pennies	45,000 pennies	45,000 pennies
42,000 pennies	42,000 pennies	42,000 pennies	42,000 pennies	42,000 pennies
38,000 pennies	38,000 pennies	38,000 pennies	38,000 pennies	38,000 pennies

33 Comb Again?

THE STORY

Teddy, Toula, Tammy, Terry and Tyree were five beachcombers. They all combed different beaches of different sizes. The beaches were 10,560, 10,200, 9,000, 8,400 and 7,200 feet long. One recent day, the five beachcombers got together and compared what they had collected over the past month. They had collected 2,400, 2,280, 2,160, 2,040 and 1,800 sea shells. They had collected 1,200, 1,140, 1,030, 900 and 630 curious stones. They had collected 56, 50, 49, 48 and 40 coins. Based on the clues, match the names with the size of the beaches they combed, and the number of seashells, stones and coins they collected.

THE CLUES

1. Toula, Tammy, Terry and Tyree each were at the top of one of the four categories and each was at the bottom of one of the four categories.
2. Between the two of them, Teddy and Toula combed 6,920 yards of beach and found 88 coins.
3. Multiply Toula's coin total by 30 to discover Terry's stone total, and multiply Toula's coin total by 45 to unearth Terry's shell total.
4. Tyree did not comb the shortest beach and he did not collect the most shells.
5. Terry found exactly 1 more coin than Tammy, and Tyree's beach was longer than Terry's beach.
6. Toula collected more stones than Teddy, but Tammy collected more stones than Toula.
7. Toula collected more shells than Teddy but less than Tyree.

Teddy	Toula	Tammy	Terry	Tyree
10,560 feet	10,560 feet	10,560 feet	10,560 feet	10,560 feet
10,200 feet	10,200 feet	10,200 feet	10,200 feet	10,200 feet
9,000 feet	9,000 feet	9,000 feet	9,000 feet	9,000 feet
8,400 feet	8,400 feet	8,400 feet	8,400 feet	8,400 feet
7,200 feet	7,200 feet	7,200 feet	7,200 feet	7,200 feet
2,400 shells	2,400 shells	2,400 shells	2,400 shells	2,400 shells
2,280 shells	2,280 shells	2,280 shells	2,280 shells	2,280 shells
2,160 shells	2,160 shells	2,160 shells	2,160 shells	2,160 shells
2,040 shells	2,040 shells	2,040 shells	2,040 shells	2,040 shells
1,800 shells	1,800 shells	1,800 shells	1,800 shells	1,800 shells
1,200 stones	1,200 stones	1,200 stones	1,200 stones	1,200 stones
1,140 stones	1,140 stones	1,140 stones	1,140 stones	1,140 stones
1,030 stones	1,030 stones	1,030 stones	1,030 stones	1,030 stones
900 stones	900 stones	900 stones	900 stones	900 stones
630 stones	630 stones	630 stones	630 stones	630 stones
56 coins	56 coins	56 coins	56 coins	56 coins
50 coins	50 coins	50 coins	50 coins	50 coins
49 coins	49 coins	49 coins	49 coins	49 coins
48 coins	48 coins	48 coins	48 coins	48 coins
40 coins	40 coins	40 coins	40 coins	40 coins

34 Don't Toy With Me

THE STORY

Mike, Mabel, Mary, Mack and Myra all were the proud owners of toy stores. Recently, they held a competition to see who could sell the most dolls, games, balls and puzzles in a week. They sold 155, 150, 140, 139 and 138 dolls. They sold 200, 195, 180, 175 and 160 games. They sold 650, 640, 630, 625 and 575 balls. They sold 75, 70, 60, 50 and 35 puzzles. Based on the clues, match the owners with the number of dolls, games, balls and puzzles they sold the week of the competition.

THE CLUES

1. Mike and Mabel each sold the most of two of the four items, and they each sold the fewest of two of the four items.
2. Multiply the number of puzzles Mary sold by 4 to determine the number of games Mike sold.
3. Mack sold exactly 1 more doll than Myra, but Myra sold exactly 1 more doll than Mike.
4. Mike sold more balls than Mary.
5. Mack sold three times as many games as puzzles, and Myra sold more games than Mary.
6. Mary sold exactly 10 more balls than Mack.

Mike	Mabel	Mary	Mack	Myra
155 dolls	155 dolls	155 dolls	155 dolls	155 dolls
150 dolls	150 dolls	150 dolls	150 dolls	150 dolls
140 dolls	140 dolls	140 dolls	140 dolls	140 dolls
139 dolls	139 dolls	139 dolls	139 dolls	139 dolls
138 dolls	138 dolls	138 dolls	138 dolls	138 dolls
200 games	200 games	200 games	200 games	200 games
195 games	195 games	195 games	195 games	195 games
180 games	180 games	180 games	180 games	180 games
175 games	175 games	175 games	175 games	175 games
160 games	160 games	160 games	160 games	160 games
650 balls	650 balls	650 balls	650 balls	650 balls
640 balls	640 balls	640 balls	640 balls	640 balls
630 balls	630 balls	630 balls	630 balls	630 balls
625 balls	625 balls	625 balls	625 balls	625 balls
575 balls	575 balls	575 balls	575 balls	575 balls
75 puzzles	75 puzzles	75 puzzles	75 puzzles	75 puzzles
70 puzzles	70 puzzles	70 puzzles	70 puzzles	70 puzzles
60 puzzles	60 puzzles	60 puzzles	60 puzzles	60 puzzles
50 puzzles	50 puzzles	50 puzzles	50 puzzles	50 puzzles
35 puzzles	35 puzzles	35 puzzles	35 puzzles	35 puzzles

35 Spare No Expense

THE STORY

Five recently married brides named Alice, Amy, Annie, Ava and Arlene compared how much they had each spent on flowers, a wedding dress, food, and a band for their weddings. They spent $27,000, $23,000, $22,000, $18,000 and $10,000 for flowers. They spent $27,000, $23,000, $22,000, $18,000 and $10,000 for a wedding dress. They spent $27,000, $23,000, $22,000, $18,000 and $10,000 for food for their wedding receptions. They spent $27,000, $23,000, $22,000, $18,000 and $10,000 for a band to provide music at their wedding receptions. Based on the clues, match the brides with the amount of money they spent for flowers, wedding dresses, food and bands.

THE CLUES

1. Annie and Ava spent a combined total of $40,000 for flowers, which was the total amount Arlene spent for her entire wedding.
2. Alice, Amy, Annie and Ava each spent a total of $90,000 for their weddings and, of course, none of them spent the same amount for more than one item.
3. Annie and Ava spent a combined total of $40,000 for food.
4. Alice paid more for her dress than Amy, and Ava spent more for her dress than Annie.
5. Amy spent more for food than Alice, and Ava spent more for flowers than Annie.

Alice	Amy	Annie	Ava	Arlene
$27,000 flowers	$27,000 flowers	$27,000 flowers	$27,000 flowers	$27,000 flowers
$23,000 flowers	$23,000 flowers	$23,000 flowers	$23,000 flowers	$23,000 flowers
$22,000 flowers	$22,000 flowers	$22,000 flowers	$22,000 flowers	$22,000 flowers
$18,000 flowers	$18,000 flowers	$18,000 flowers	$18,000 flowers	$18,000 flowers
$10,000 flowers	$10,000 flowers	$10,000 flowers	$10,000 flowers	$10,000 flowers
$27,000 dress	$27,000 dress	$27,000 dress	$27,000 dress	$27,000 dress
$23,000 dress	$23,000 dress	$23,000 dress	$23,000 dress	$23,000 dress
$22,000 dress	$22,000 dress	$22,000 dress	$22,000 dress	$22,000 dress
$18,000 dress	$18,000 dress	$18,000 dress	$18,000 dress	$18,000 dress
$10,000 dress	$10,000 dress	$10,000 dress	$10,000 dress	$10,000 dress
$27,000 food	$27,000 food	$27,000 food	$27,000 food	$27,000 food
$23,000 food	$23,000 food	$23,000 food	$23,000 food	$23,000 food
$22,000 food	$22,000 food	$22,000 food	$22,000 food	$22,000 food
$18,000 food	$18,000 food	$18,000 food	$18,000 food	$18,000 food
$10,000 food	$10,000 food	$10,000 food	$10,000 food	$10,000 food
$27,000 band	$27,000 band	$27,000 band	$27,000 band	$27,000 band
$23,000 band	$23,000 band	$23,000 band	$23,000 band	$23,000 band
$22,000 band	$22,000 band	$22,000 band	$22,000 band	$22,000 band
$18,000 band	$18,000 band	$18,000 band	$18,000 band	$18,000 band
$10,000 band	$10,000 band	$10,000 band	$10,000 band	$10,000 band

36 Swinging Shoppers

THE STORY

Five monkeys named Jerry, Willie, Nicky, Calvin and Bogey went on a shopping spree. They visited 22, 20, 18, 17 and 15 stores. They purchased 83, 81, 80, 79 and 75 pairs of pants. They purchased 27, 23, 19, 15 and 10 pairs of shoes. They purchased 58, 55, 45, 40 and 30 shirts. Based on the clues, match the monkeys with the number of stores they visited, and the number of pants, pairs of shoes and shirts they purchased.

THE CLUES

1. Jerry, Willie and Calvin each bought the most of one of the three clothing items, and each bought the fewest of one of the three clothing items.
2. Nicky and Calvin visited a combined total of 42 stores, and Willie and Bogey visited a combined total of 32 stores.
3. Multiply the pairs of shoes Jerry bought by 8 to reveal the number of pants Bogey bought.
4. Calvin bought more pants than Jerry, and Jerry bought more pants than Nicky.
5. Willie and Nicky bought a combined total of 50 pairs of shoes, and Jerry and Bogey bought a combined total of 25 pairs of shoes.
6. Nicky bought exactly 5 more shirts than Willie, and Bogey visited more stores than Willie.
7. The monkey that bought the fewest shirts visited the most stores.

Jerry	Willie	Nicky	Calvin	Bogey
22 stores	22 stores	22 stores	22 stores	22 stores
20 stores	20 stores	20 stores	20 stores	20 stores
18 stores	18 stores	18 stores	18 stores	18 stores
17 stores	17 stores	17 stores	17 stores	17 stores
15 stores	15 stores	15 stores	15 stores	15 stores
83 pants	83 pants	83 pants	83 pants	83 pants
81 pants	81 pants	81 pants	81 pants	81 pants
80 pants	80 pants	80 pants	80 pants	80 pants
79 pants	79 pants	79 pants	79 pants	79 pants
75 pants	75 pants	75 pants	75 pants	75 pants
27 shoe pairs	27 shoe pairs	27 shoe pairs	27 shoe pairs	27 shoe pairs
23 shoe pairs	23 shoe pairs	23 shoe pairs	23 shoe pairs	23 shoe pairs
19 shoe pairs	19 shoe pairs	19 shoe pairs	19 shoe pairs	19 shoe pairs
15 shoe pairs	15 shoe pairs	15 shoe pairs	15 shoe pairs	15 shoe pairs
10 shoe pairs	10 shoe pairs	10 shoe pairs	10 shoe pairs	10 shoe pairs
58 shirts	58 shirts	58 shirts	58 shirts	58 shirts
55 shirts	55 shirts	55 shirts	55 shirts	55 shirts
45 shirts	45 shirts	45 shirts	45 shirts	45 shirts
40 shirts	40 shirts	40 shirts	40 shirts	40 shirts
30 shirts	30 shirts	30 shirts	30 shirts	30 shirts

37 De Sign! De Sign!

THE STORY

Five clothing designers named Nicky, Vickie, Claude, Patty and Pierre recently went to a fabric store and bought material to be used in the creation of their new collections. They purchased 100, 90, 85, 80 and 75 yards of silk. They purchased 100, 90, 85, 80 and 75 yards of cotton. They purchased 100, 90, 85, 80 and 75 yards of satin. They purchased 100, 90, 85, 80 and 75 yards of linen. Based on the clues, match the designers with the amount of silk, cotton, satin and linen they purchased.

THE CLUES

1. Nicky bought equal amounts of satin and linen, Vickie bought equal amounts of satin and linen, and Claude bought equal amounts of satin and linen.
2. Patty bought the most of two out of the four fabrics and she bought the least of two out of the four fabrics, but Pierre also bought the most of two out of the four fabrics and he bought the least of two out of the four fabrics.
3. Nicky bought 30 feet more cotton than silk, and Claude bought more silk than Vickie.
4. Claude and Patty bought a combined total of 570 feet of silk, and Nicky and Pierre bought a combined total of 570 feet of cotton.
5. Claude bought more cotton than Vickie, and Vickie bought more satin than Claude.
6. Neither Nicky's silk number nor his cotton number was the same as his satin number.
7. Pierre bought more satin than Patty.

Nicky	Vickie	Claude	Patty	Pierre
100 yds. silk	100 yds. silk	100 yds. silk	100 yds. silk	100 yds. silk
90 yds. silk	90 yds. silk	90 yds. silk	90 yds. silk	90 yds. silk
85 yds. silk	85 yds. silk	85 yds. silk	85 yds. silk	85 yds. silk
80 yds. silk	80 yds. silk	80 yds. silk	80 yds. silk	80 yds. silk
75 yds. silk	75 yds. silk	75 yds. silk	75 yds. silk	75 yds. silk
100 yds. cotton	100 yds. cotton	100 yds. cotton	100 yds. cotton	100 yds. cotton
90 yds. cotton	90 yds. cotton	90 yds. cotton	90 yds. cotton	90 yds. cotton
85 yds. cotton	85 yds. cotton	85 yds. cotton	85 yds. cotton	85 yds. cotton
80 yds. cotton	80 yds. cotton	80 yds. cotton	80 yds. cotton	80 yds. cotton
75 yds. cotton	75 yds. cotton	75 yds. cotton	75 yds. cotton	75 yds. cotton
100 yds. satin	100 yds. satin	100 yds. satin	100 yds. satin	100 yds. satin
90 yds. satin	90 yds. satin	90 yds. satin	90 yds. satin	90 yds. satin
85 yds. satin	85 yds. satin	85 yds. satin	85 yds. satin	85 yds. satin
80 yds. satin	80 yds. satin	80 yds. satin	80 yds. satin	80 yds. satin
75 yds. satin	75 yds. satin	75 yds. satin	75 yds. satin	75 yds. satin
100 yds. linen	100 yds. linen	100 yds. linen	100 yds. linen	100 yds. linen
90 yds. linen	90 yds. linen	90 yds. linen	90 yds. linen	90 yds. linen
85 yds. linen	85 yds. linen	85 yds. linen	85 yds. linen	85 yds. linen
80 yds. linen	80 yds. linen	80 yds. linen	80 yds. linen	80 yds. linen
75 yds. linen	75 yds. linen	75 yds. linen	75 yds. linen	75 yds. linen

38 Library Business

THE STORY

The librarians for the towns of Alpha, Beta, Crown, Dofuss and Enid got together recently to discuss library business. In a recent week, they had 1,000, 990, 980, 975 and 950 visitors to their libraries. They had loaned out 3,000, 2,500, 1,960, 1,950 and 1,900 books. Their overdue book totals were 9,900, 9,800, 9,750, 9,500 and 9,000. To ensure order in their libraries, the librarians had on display 500, 475, 450, 400 and 300 quiet signs. Based on the clues, match the towns with their library visitors, books loaned, books overdue and quiet signs.

THE CLUES

1. Beta and Crown each had the highest numbers in two of the four categories, and Dofuss and Enid each had the lowest number in two of the four categories.
2. Alpha and Beta had a combined total of 975 quiet signs on display, and Beta and Dofuss had a combined total of 18,500 overdue books.
3. Beta did not loan out the most books that week, Enid had exactly 25 more visitors than Dofuss, and Crown had more visitors than Alpha.
4. Dofuss and Enid had a combined total of 700 quiet signs on display.
5. Beta and Enid had a combined total of 19,300 overdue books.
6. Alpha loaned out fewer books than Beta, and Beta loaned out fewer books than Dofuss.

Alpha	Beta	Crown	Dofuss	Enid
1,000 visitors	1,000 visitors	1,000 visitors	1,000 visitors	1,000 visitors
990 visitors	990 visitors	990 visitors	990 visitors	990 visitors
980 visitors	980 visitors	980 visitors	980 visitors	980 visitors
975 visitors	975 visitors	975 visitors	975 visitors	975 visitors
950 visitors	950 visitors	950 visitors	950 visitors	950 visitors
3,000 loans	3,000 loans	3,000 loans	3,000 loans	3,000 loans
2,500 loans	2,500 loans	2,500 loans	2,500 loans	2,500 loans
1,960 loans	1,960 loans	1,960 loans	1,960 loans	1,960 loans
1,950 loans	1,950 loans	1,950 loans	1,950 loans	1,950 loans
1,900 loans	1,900 loans	1,900 loans	1,900 loans	1,900 loans
9,900 overdue	9,900 overdue	9,900 overdue	9,900 overdue	9,900 overdue
9,800 overdue	9,800 overdue	9,800 overdue	9,800 overdue	9,800 overdue
9,750 overdue	9,750 overdue	9,750 overdue	9,750 overdue	9,750 overdue
9,500 overdue	9,500 overdue	9,500 overdue	9,500 overdue	9,500 overdue
9,000 overdue	9,000 overdue	9,000 overdue	9,000 overdue	9,000 overdue
500 signs	500 signs	500 signs	500 signs	500 signs
475 signs	475 signs	475 signs	475 signs	475 signs
450 signs	450 signs	450 signs	450 signs	450 signs
400 signs	400 signs	400 signs	400 signs	400 signs
300 signs	300 signs	300 signs	300 signs	300 signs

39 Video Business

THE STORY

Albert, Betty, Connie, Dwayne and Elvis all owned video stores. Recently, they compared rentals of the four most popular types of DVDs. In one week, they rented out 4,500, 4,400, 4,000, 3,800 and 3,500 comedies. They rented out 9,000, 8,800, 8,000, 7,000 and 6,500 thrillers. They rented out 6,000, 5,500, 5,000, 4,000 and 3,000 action DVDs. They rented out 700, 650, 450, 400 and 350 musicals. Based on the clues, match the store owners with the number of comedy, thriller, action and musical DVDs they rented out that week.

THE CLUES

1. Albert, Betty and Elvis rented out the three lowest numbers of comedies.
2. Multiply Dwayne's musical rental number by 10 to find his comedy rental number.
3. Multiply Elvis' musical rental number by 10 to reveal his thriller rental number.
4. Multiply Albert's musical rental number by 10 to discover the number of both his comedy and action rental numbers.
5. Elvis' comedy rental number was one-half the size of his thriller rental number.
6. Multiply Betty's musical rental number by 10 to identify her thriller rental number.
7. Elvis rented exactly 2,000 more action DVDs than Dwayne.
8. Dwayne's action movie rental number was one-third the size of his thriller number.
9. Betty rented more action movies than Connie, and Connie rented more thrillers than Albert.

Albert	Betty	Connie	Dwayne	Elvis
4,500 comedy	4,500 comedy	4,500 comedy	4,500 comedy	4,500 comedy
4,400 comedy	4,400 comedy	4,400 comedy	4,400 comedy	4,400 comedy
4,000 comedy	4,000 comedy	4,000 comedy	4,000 comedy	4,000 comedy
3,800 comedy	3,800 comedy	3,800 comedy	3,800 comedy	3,800 comedy
3,500 comedy	3,500 comedy	3,500 comedy	3,500 comedy	3,500 comedy
9,000 thriller	9,000 thriller	9,000 thriller	9,000 thriller	9,000 thriller
8,800 thriller	8,800 thriller	8,800 thriller	8,800 thriller	8,800 thriller
8,000 thriller	8,000 thriller	8,000 thriller	8,000 thriller	8,000 thriller
7,000 thriller	7,000 thriller	7,000 thriller	7,000 thriller	7,000 thriller
6,500 thriller	6,500 thriller	6,500 thriller	6,500 thriller	6,500 thriller
6,000 action	6,000 action	6,000 action	6,000 action	6,000 action
5,500 action	5,500 action	5,500 action	5,500 action	5,500 action
5,000 action	5,000 action	5,000 action	5,000 action	5,000 action
4,000 action	4,000 action	4,000 action	4,000 action	4,000 action
3,000 action	3,000 action	3,000 action	3,000 action	3,000 action
700 music	700 music	700 music	700 music	700 music
650 music	650 music	650 music	650 music	650 music
450 music	450 music	450 music	450 music	450 music
400 music	400 music	400 music	400 music	400 music
350 music	350 music	350 music	350 music	350 music

40 Time For A Change?

THE STORY

Five wizards named Goro, Harlow, Chico, Zero and Gino were very proud of their ability to cast spells. One recent day, they decided to have a contest to see who could change the most people into different kinds of animals. They changed 200, 190, 150, 110 and 90 people into rats. They changed 170, 160, 140, 130 and 90 people into bats. They changed 75, 70, 65, 60 and 50 people into cats. They changed 25, 20, 15, 10 and 5 people into newts. Based on the clues, match the wizards with the number of people they changed into rats, bats, cats and newts.

THE CLUES

1. Chico and Zero together changed 390 people into rats, 330 people into bats, 145 people into cats, and 45 people into newts.
2. Goro and Harlow together changed 200 people into rats, 220 people into bats, 110 people into cats, and 15 people into newts.
3. Harlow changed a total of 310 people into rats, bats, cats and newts.
4. Chico changed 160 more people into rats, bats, cats and newts than Harlow.

Goro	Harlow	Chico	Zero	Gino
200 rats	200 rats	200 rats	200 rats	200 rats
190 rats	190 rats	190 rats	190 rats	190 rats
150 rats	150 rats	150 rats	150 rats	150 rats
110 rats	110 rats	110 rats	110 rats	110 rats
90 rats	90 rats	90 rats	90 rats	90 rats
170 bats	170 bats	170 bats	170 bats	170 bats
160 bats	160 bats	160 bats	160 bats	160 bats
140 bats	140 bats	140 bats	140 bats	140 bats
130 bats	130 bats	130 bats	130 bats	130 bats
90 bats	90 bats	90 bats	90 bats	90 bats
75 cats	75 cats	75 cats	75 cats	75 cats
70 cats	70 cats	70 cats	70 cats	70 cats
65 cats	65 cats	65 cats	65 cats	65 cats
60 cats	60 cats	60 cats	60 cats	60 cats
50 cats	50 cats	50 cats	50 cats	50 cats
25 newts	25 newts	25 newts	25 newts	25 newts
20 newts	20 newts	20 newts	20 newts	20 newts
15 newts	15 newts	15 newts	15 newts	15 newts
10 newts	10 newts	10 newts	10 newts	10 newts
5 newts	5 newts	5 newts	5 newts	5 newts

41 Time Travels

THE STORY

In the year 2005, five time travelers got together to compare their time travels. Their names were Nate, Nancy, Neil, Nellie and Ned, and in the year 2005 they were 40, 39, 38, 35 and 30 years old. As of the year 2005, they had made one trip forward in time to the years 3000, 2990, 2505, 2400 and 2105. As of the year 2005, they all had made one trip back in time to the years 1900, 1850, 1800, 1775 and 1750. As of the year 2005, the total number of years each time traveler had traveled backward and forward in time was 1,250, 1,215, 705, 550 and 205 years. Based on the clues, match the names with their ages, the dates they traveled forward to, the dates they traveled backward to, and the total number of years each time traveler had traveled forward and backward in time.

THE CLUES

1. As of 2005, Nancy was exactly 5 years older than Nate, Nellie was exactly 5 years older than Nancy, and Ned was a year younger than Nellie.
2. As of 2005, Nate and Nancy traveled a combined total of 1,980 years into the future, and Neil and Nellie traveled a combined total of 895 years into the future.
3. As of 2005, Nate and Nancy traveled a combined total of 485 years into the past, and Nellie and Ned traveled a combined total of 260 years into the past.
4. As of 2005, Ned traveled the least total span of years traveling in time, and Nate traveled the greatest total span of years time traveling.

Nate	Nancy	Neil	Nellie	Ned
age 40	age 40	age 40	age 40	age 40
age 39	age 39	age 39	age 39	age 39
age 38	age 38	age 38	age 38	age 38
age 35	age 35	age 35	age 35	age 35
age 30	age 30	age 30	age 30	age 30
year 3000	year 3000	year 3000	year 3000	year 3000
year 2990	year 2990	year 2990	year 2990	year 2990
year 2505	year 2505	year 2505	year 2505	year 2505
year 2400	year 2400	year 2400	year 2400	year 2400
year 2105	year 2105	year 2105	year 2105	year 2105
year 1900	year 1900	year 1900	year 1900	year 1900
year 1850	year 1850	year 1850	year 1850	year 1850
year 1800	year 1800	year 1800	year 1800	year 1800
year 1775	year 1775	year 1775	year 1775	year 1775
year 1750	year 1750	year 1750	year 1759	year 1750
1,250 total	1,250 total	1,250 total	1,250 total	1,250 total
1,215 total	1,215 total	1,215 total	1,215 total	1,215 total
705 total	705 total	705 total	705 total	705 total
550 total	550 total	550 total	550 total	550 total
205 total	205 total	205 total	205 total	205 total

42 Lumbering Along

THE STORY

Alice, Betty, Calvin, David and Eric were lumberjacks who enjoyed competing against each other. Their ages were 60, 50, 30, 25 and 20 years old. They entered the annual greased pole-climbing contest held in the Glenview forest and climbed 90, 84, 78, 75 and 63 feet before sliding down without reaching the top of the pole. After the contest, they bragged about the biggest trees they chopped down. The trees were 72, 68, 36, 34 and 30 inches in diameter. They then bragged about the biggest pancakes they had eaten. The pancakes were 50, 46, 40, 18 and 17 inches in diameter. Based on the clues, match the lumberjacks with their ages, their greased pole heights, their tree diameters, and the diameter of their pancakes.

THE CLUES

1. The radius of Betty's tree was the same as the diameter of Calvin's tree, and the diameter of David's tree was the same as the radius of Alice's tree, and the diameter of Alice's pancake was the same as the radius of David's tree, and the diameter of Betty's pancake was the same as the radius of Calvin's tree.
2. Calvin was one-half the age of Betty, Eric was one-half the age of Alice, and David was one-third Betty's age.
3. Alice climbed the greased pole exactly 2 yards less than David and exactly 4 yards less than Eric.
4. David's age was the same as his pancake radius, and Eric's pancake radius was the same as his age.
5. Calvin was the worst pole climber, and the oldest lumberjack chopped down the biggest tree.

Alice	Betty	Calvin	David	Eric
age 60	age 60	age 60	age 60	age 60
age 50	age 50	age 50	age 50	age 50
age 30	age 30	age 30	age 30	age 30
age 25	age 25	age 25	age 25	age 25
age 20	age 20	age 20	age 20	age 20
90 feet	90 feet	90 feet	90 feet	90 feet
84 feet	84 feet	84 feet	84 feet	84 feet
78 feet	78 feet	78 feet	78 feet	78 feet
75 feet	75 feet	75 feet	75 feet	75 feet
63 feet	63 feet	63 feet	63 feet	63 feet
72 in. tree	72 in. tree	72 in. tree	72 in. tree	72 in. tree
68 in. tree	68 in. tree	68 in. tree	68 in. tree	68 in. tree
36 in. tree	36 in. tree	36 in. tree	36 in. tree	36 in. tree
34 in. tree	34 in. tree	34 in. tree	34 in. tree	34 in. tree
30 in. tree	30 in. tree	30 in. tree	30 in. tree	30 in. tree
50 in. pancake	50 in. pancake	50 in. pancake	50 in. pancake	50 in. pancake
46 in. pancake	46 in. pancake	46 in. pancake	46 in. pancake	46 in. pancake
40 in. pancake	40 in. pancake	40 in. pancake	40 in. pancake	40 in. pancake
18 in. pancake	18 in. pancake	18 in. pancake	18 in. pancake	18 in. pancake
17 in. pancake	17 in. pancake	17 in. pancake	17 in. pancake	17 in. pancake

43 Town Rectangles

THE STORY

The towns of Alpha, Beta, Crown, Dofuss and Enid all had town rectangles in the center of their towns where the citizens could gather to sing and give each other flowers. The town rectangles were 300, 291, 282, 276 and 255 feet in length, and 201, 174, 150, 126 and 99 feet wide. The towns all had round town towers of exactly the same height but of different diameters. The diameters of the towers were 20, 18, 16, 10 and 9 feet. Based on the clues, match the towns with the length, width and total square area of their rectangles, and the diameters of their round town towers.

THE CLUES

1. The radius of the Dofuss tower was the same as the diameter of the Alpha tower, and the diameter of the Beta tower was the same as the radius of Crown's tower.
2. Dofuss' rectangle length was exactly 15 yards less than Enid's rectangle length, which was one reason why Enid's rectangle area was the largest and Dofuss' rectangle area was the smallest.
3. Crown's width was 8 yards more than Beta's width, and Alpha's width was 8 yards less than Beta's width.
4. Of course, Beta's length was 3 yards less than Enid's length, and Beta's tower was smaller than Alpha's tower.

Alpha	Beta	Crown	Dofuss	Enid
300 ft. length	300 ft. length	300 ft. length	300 ft. length	300 ft. length
291 ft. length	291 ft. length	291 ft. length	291 ft. length	291 ft. length
282 ft. length	282 ft. length	282 ft. length	282 ft. length	282 ft. length
276 ft. length	276 ft. length	276 ft. length	276 ft. length	276 ft. length
255 ft. length	255 ft. length	255 ft. length	255 ft. length	255 ft. length
201 ft. width	201 ft. width	201 ft. width	201 ft. width	201 ft. width
174 ft. width	174 ft. width	174 ft. width	174 ft. width	174 ft. width
150 ft. width	150 ft. width	150 ft. width	150 ft. width	150 ft. width
126 ft. width	126 ft. width	126 ft. width	126 ft. width	126 ft. width
99 ft. width	99 ft. width	99 ft. width	99 ft. width	99 ft. width
6,700 sq. yds.	6,700 sq. yds.	6,700 sq. yds.	6,700 sq. yds.	6,700 sq. yds.
5,452 sq. yds.	5,452 sq. yds.	5,452 sq. yds.	5,452 sq. yds.	5,452 sq. yds.
4,850 sq. yds.	4,850 sq. yds.	4,850 sq. yds.	4,850 sq. yds.	4,850 sq. yds.
3,864 sq. yds.	3,864 sq. yds.	3,864 sq. yds.	3,864 sq. yds.	3,864 sq. yds.
2,805 sq. yds.	2,805 sq. yds.	2,805 sq. yds.	2,805 sq. yds.	2,805 sq. yds.
20 ft. tower	20 ft. tower	20 ft. tower	20 ft. tower	20 ft. tower
18 ft. tower	18 ft. tower	18 ft. tower	18 ft. tower	18 ft. tower
16 ft. tower	16 ft. tower	16 ft. tower	16 ft. tower	16 ft. tower
10 ft. tower	10 ft. tower	10 ft. tower	10 ft. tower	10 ft. tower
9 ft. tower	9 ft. tower	9 ft. tower	9 ft. tower	9 ft. tower

44 A Fortune In Cookies

THE STORY

The Adams, Bates, Twain, Wilson and Taft schools all held their annual fund raising bake sales. They sold 10,800, 10,680, 10,200, 9,900 and 9,000 cookies. They sold 9,120, 8,880, 8,868, 8,808 and 8,760 cupcakes. They sold 7,776, 7,740, 7,680, 7,668 and 7,620 doughnuts. They sold 3,780, 3,756, 3,720, 3,696 and 3,600 brownies. Based on the clues, match the schools with their sales of cookies, cupcakes, doughnuts and brownies.

THE CLUES

1. The Adams, Bates and Twain schools sold a combined total of 2,640 dozen cookies, 2,239 dozen cupcakes, 1,933 dozen doughnuts, and 938 dozen brownies.
2. The Bates School sold more cookies than Adams, more cupcakes than Twain, more doughnuts than Adams, and more brownies than Twain.
3. The Adams School sold more cookies and doughnuts than the Twain School, but the Twain School sold more cupcakes and brownies than the Adams School.
4. The Taft School sold a combined total of 1,480 dozen cookies and cupcakes.
5. The Wilson School did not sell the fewest doughnuts or brownies.

Adams	Bates	Twain	Wilson	Taft
10,800 cookies	10,800 cookies	10,800 cookies	10,800 cookies	10,800 cookies
10,680 cookies	10,680 cookies	10,680 cookies	10,680 cookies	10,680 cookies
10,200 cookies	10,200 cookies	10,200 cookies	10,200 cookies	10,200 cookies
9,900 cookies	9,900 cookies	9,900 cookies	9,900 cookies	9,900 cookies
9,000 cookies	9,000 cookies	9,000 cookies	9,000 cookies	9,000 cookies
9,120 cupcakes	9,120 cupcakes	9,120 cupcakes	9,120 cupcakes	9,120 cupcakes
8,880 cupcakes	8,880 cupcakes	8,880 cupcakes	8,880 cupcakes	8,880 cupcakes
8,868 cupcakes	8,868 cupcakes	8,868 cupcakes	8,868 cupcakes	8,868 cupcakes
8,808 cupcakes	8,808 cupcakes	8,808 cupcakes	8,808 cupcakes	8,808 cupcakes
8,760 cupcakes	8,760 cupcakes	8,760 cupcakes	8,760 cupcakes	8,760 cupcakes
7,776 doughnuts	7,776 doughnuts	7,776 doughnuts	7,776 doughnuts	7,776 doughnuts
7,740 doughnuts	7,740 doughnuts	7,740 doughnuts	7,740 doughnuts	7,740 doughnuts
7,680 doughnuts	7,680 doughnuts	7,680 doughnuts	7,680 doughnuts	7,680 doughnuts
7,668 doughnuts	7,668 doughnuts	7,668 doughnuts	7,668 doughnuts	7,668 doughnuts
7,620 doughnuts	7,620 doughnuts	7,620 doughnuts	7,620 doughnuts	7,620 doughnuts
3,780 brownies	3,780 brownies	3,780 brownies	3,780 brownies	3,780 brownies
3,756 brownies	3,756 brownies	3,756 brownies	3,756 brownies	3,756 brownies
3,720 brownies	3,720 brownies	3,720 brownies	3,720 brownies	3,720 brownies
3,696 brownies	3,696 brownies	3,696 brownies	3,696 brownies	3,696 brownies
3,600 brownies	3,600 brownies	3,600 brownies	3,600 brownies	3,600 brownies

45 School Nurses

THE STORY

Five school nurses named Queenie, Retta, Sophie, Trudy and Vicky got together recently to discuss their jobs. In a recent month they had handed out 270, 260, 250, 200 and 150 bandages. They had handed out 425, 420, 415, 400 and 375 lozenges. They had given out 95, 90, 80, 70 and 45 ice packs. They had given out 40, 35, 30, 25 and 15 squirts of ointment. Based on the clues, match the nurses with the number of bandages, lozenges, ice packs and squirts of ointment they had administered that month.

THE CLUES

1. Queenie and Retta handed out a combined total of 530 bandages, 845 lozenges, 185 ice packs, and 75 squirts of ointment.
2. Vicky did not hand out the least of anything.
3. Trudy and Vicky handed out a combined total of 450 bandages.
4. Sophie and Trudy handed out a combined total of 775 lozenges and 125 ice packs.
5. Trudy and Vicky handed out a combined total of 45 squirts of ointment and 150 ice packs.
6. Sophie and Vicky handed out a combined total of 815 lozenges and 400 bandages.
7. Retta and Sophie handed out a combined total of 420 bandages and 825 lozenges.
8. Queenie and Trudy handed out a combined total of 175 ice packs and 55 squirts of ointment.

Queenie	Retta	Sophie	Trudy	Vicky
270 bandages	270 bandages	270 bandages	270 bandages	270 bandages
260 bandages	260 bandages	260 bandages	260 bandages	260 bandages
250 bandages	250 bandages	250 bandages	250 bandages	250 bandages
200 bandages	200 bandages	200 bandages	200 bandages	200 bandages
150 bandages	150 bandages	150 bandages	150 bandages	150 bandages
425 lozenges	425 lozenges	425 lozenges	425 lozenges	425 lozenges
420 lozenges	420 lozenges	420 lozenges	420 lozenges	420 lozenges
415 lozenges	415 lozenges	415 lozenges	415 lozenges	415 lozenges
400 lozenges	400 lozenges	400 lozenges	400 lozenges	400 lozenges
375 lozenges	375 lozenges	375 lozenges	375 lozenges	375 lozenges
95 ice packs	95 ice packs	95 ice packs	95 ice packs	95 ice packs
90 ice packs	90 ice packs	90 ice packs	90 ice packs	90 ice packs
80 ice packs	80 ice packs	80 ice packs	80 ice packs	80 ice packs
70 ice packs	70 ice packs	70 ice packs	70 ice packs	70 ice packs
45 ice packs	45 ice packs	45 ice packs	45 ice packs	45 ice packs
40 squirts	40 squirts	40 squirts	40 squirts	40 squirts
35 squirts	35 squirts	35 squirts	35 squirts	35 squirts
30 squirts	30 squirts	30 squirts	30 squirts	30 squirts
25 squirts	25 squirts	25 squirts	25 squirts	25 squirts
15 squirts	15 squirts	15 squirts	15 squirts	15 squirts

 |

46 Happy Webbing Day

THE STORY

Five spiders named Creeper, Leggy, Spot, Muffy and Fido spun webs that were 48, 36, 24, 18 and 12 inches in diameter. Recently, they got together and compared what they had captured in their webs. They caught 900, 850, 700, 450 and 425 flies. They caught 350, 225, 200, 175 and 100 moths. They caught 90, 85, 70, 45 and 30 bees. Based on the clues, match the spiders with their web's diameter, and the number of flies, moths and bees they caught.

THE CLUES

1. The diameter of Fido's web was the same as the radius of Creeper's web, the diameter of Creeper's web was the same as the radius of Spot's web, and, of course, the radius of Muffy's web was the same as the diameter of Leggy's web.
2. Multiply Spot's bee number by 10 to find Leggy's fly number, and multiply Leggy's bee number by 10 to uncover Fido's fly number.
3. Creeper and Leggy's combined fly total was 1,750, and Muffy and Fido's combined bee total was 75.
4. Creeper did not catch the most bees, and if you multiplied Muffy's bee number by 10, the answer would be Spot's fly number.
5. Creeper and Leggy caught a combined total of 575 moths, and Muffy and Fido caught a combined total of 275 moths.
6. Creeper's moth number was one-half of Fido's fly number, and Muffy's moth number was one-half Spot's moth number.

Creeper	Leggy	Spot	Muffy	Fido
48 inches	48 inches	48 inches	48 inches	48 inches
36 inches	36 inches	36 inches	36 inches	36 inches
24 inches	24 inches	24 inches	24 inches	24 inches
18 inches	18 inches	18 inches	18 inches	18 inches
12 inches	12 inches	12 inches	12 inches	12 inches
900 flies	900 flies	900 flies	900 flies	900 flies
850 flies	850 flies	850 flies	850 flies	850 flies
700 flies	700 flies	700 flies	700 flies	700 flies
450 flies	450 flies	450 flies	450 flies	450 flies
425 flies	425 flies	425 flies	425 flies	425 flies
350 moths	350 moths	350 moths	350 moths	350 moths
225 moths	225 moths	225 moths	225 moths	225 moths
200 moths	200 moths	200 moths	200 moths	200 moths
175 moths	175 moths	175 moths	175 moths	175 moths
100 moths	100 moths	100 moths	100 moths	100 moths
90 bees	90 bees	90 bees	90 bees	90 bees
85 bees	85 bees	85 bees	85 bees	85 bees
70 bees	70 bees	70 bees	70 bees	70 bees
45 bees	45 bees	45 bees	45 bees	45 bees
30 bees	30 bees	30 bees	30 bees	30 bees

47 Jockey Careers

THE STORY

Five jockeys named Tom, Jerry, Mutt, Jeff and Curley had the most unusual four-year careers in horse racing history. In their four year careers the five jockeys all placed exactly 120 times. Except for one jockey who finished in exactly the same place for all four years, the other four jockeys always finished in the same place in one year but a different place in another year without ever repeating a place. The jockeys always finished in 1st, 2nd, 3rd, 4th and 5th place in each of the four years of their careers. Based on the clues, find the one jockey who finished in the same place the same number of times for all four years, and the places of the remaining four jockeys for the four years.

THE CLUES

1. Except for one jockey who finished in the same place all four years, the other jockeys all spent one of the four years in the same place only once.
2. In the first year, Tom and Jerry finished in a combined total of 90 races and in the second year, they finished in a combined total of 90 races.
3. In the third year, Jeff and Curley finished in a combined total of 90 races.
4. In the first year, Mutt finished in as many races as Jeff and Curley did together, and the same thing happened in the second year.
5. In the first year, Jerry finished more races than Tom, and Jeff finished more races than Curley.
6. In the fourth year, Tom finished more races than Jerry, and Curley finished more races than Jeff.

	Tom	Jerry	Mutt	Jeff	Curley
YEAR 1	1st place 10	1st place 10	1st place 10	1st place 10	1st place 10
	2nd place 20	2nd place 20	2nd place 20	2nd place 20	2nd place 20
	3rd place 30	3rd place 30	3rd place 30	3rd place 30	3rd place 30
	4th place 40	4th place 40	4th place 40	4th place 40	4th place 40
	5th place 50	5th place 50	5th place 50	5th place 50	5th place 50
YEAR 2	1st place 10	1st place 10	1st place 10	1st place 10	1st place 10
	2nd place 20	2nd place 20	2nd place 20	2nd place 20	2nd place 20
	3rd place 30	3rd place 30	3rd place 30	3rd place 30	3rd place 30
	4th place 40	4th place 40	4th place 40	4th place 40	4th place 40
	5th place 50	5th place 50	5th place 50	5th place 50	5th place 50
YEAR 3	1st place 10	1st place 10	1st place 10	1st place 10	1st place 10
	2nd place 20	2nd place 20	2nd place 20	2nd place 20	2nd place 20
	3rd place 30	3rd place 30	3rd place 30	3rd place 30	3rd place 30
	4th place 40	4th place 40	4th place 40	4th place 40	4th place 40
	5th place 50	5th place 50	5th place 50	5th place 50	5th place 50
YEAR 4	1st place 10	1st place 10	1st place 10	1st place 10	1st place 10
	2nd place 20	2nd place 20	2nd place 20	2nd place 20	2nd place 20
	3rd place 30	3rd place 30	3rd place 30	3rd place 30	3rd place 30
	4th place 40	4th place 40	4th place 40	4th place 40	4th place 40
	5th place 50	5th place 50	5th place 50	5th place 50	5th place 50

48 Cone Heads

THE STORY

Alice, Belle, Carol, Dale and Evelyn were standing in line at an ice cream store waiting to buy ice cream. They were 30, 35, 50, 60 and 70 years old. Naturally, they were 1st, 2nd, 3rd, 4th and 5th place in line. They ordered 1, 2, 3, 4 and 5 scoops of vanilla ice cream on their cones. They ordered 1, 2, 3, 4 and 5 scoops of peach ice cream on those same cones. Based on the clues, match the names with their ages, their places in line, and the number of scoops of vanilla and peach ice cream on their cones.

THE CLUES

1. The oldest was last in line, the next oldest was next to last, and so on to the youngest who was first in line.
2. The first in line did not take exactly 1 scoop of vanilla or peach, the second in line did not take exactly 2 scoops of vanilla or peach, and so on to the fifth in line not taking exactly 5 scoops of vanilla or peach.
3. The combined age of Carol and Dale was 65 years, and the combined age of Alice and Evelyn was 110 years.
4. While waiting in line, Dale poked Carol in the back, and Alice poked Evelyn in the back.
5. Carol and Dale had a combined total of only 3 scoops of vanilla on their cones, and Alice and Belle had a combined total of 8 scoops of vanilla and 7 scoops of peach on their cones.
6. Alice had more scoops of peach than Belle, and Dale had more scoops of peach than Carol.

Alice	Belle	Carol	Dale	Evelyn
30 years old	30 years old	30 years old	30 years old	30 years old
35 years old	35 years old	35 years old	35 years old	35 years old
50 years old	50 years old	50 years old	50 years old	50 years old
60 years old	60 years old	60 years old	60 years old	60 years old
70 years old	70 years old	70 years old	70 years old	70 years old
1st in line	1st in line	1st in line	1st in line	1st in line
2nd in line	2nd in line	2nd in line	2nd in line	2nd in line
3rd in line	3rd in line	3rd in line	3rd in line	3rd in line
4th in line	4th in line	4th in line	4th in line	4th in line
5th in line	5th in line	5th in line	5th in line	5th in line
1 vanilla	1 vanilla	1 vanilla	1 vanilla	1 vanilla
2 vanilla	2 vanilla	2 vanilla	2 vanilla	2 vanilla
3 vanilla	3 vanilla	3 vanilla	3 vanilla	3 vanilla
4 vanilla	4 vanilla	4 vanilla	4 vanilla	4 vanilla
5 vanilla	5 vanilla	5 vanilla	5 vanilla	5 vanilla
1 peach	1 peach	1 peach	1 peach	1 peach
2 peach	2 peach	2 peach	2 peach	2 peach
3 peach	3 peach	3 peach	3 peach	3 peach
4 peach	4 peach	4 peach	4 peach	4 peach
5 peach	5 peach	5 peach	5 peach	5 peach

49 Sledding With Dogs

THE STORY

Helen, Hayley, Greg, George and June all entered a 1,000 mile dog sled race. None of the five finished the race and they dropped out after racing 800, 600, 500, 300 and 200 miles. During the race, they all got lost for 17, 16, 14, 10 and 7 days. Amazingly, they had dog teams of 17, 16, 14, 10 and 7 dogs. All the racers lost weight during the race and they lost 17, 16, 14, 10 and 7 pounds. Based on the clues, match the racers with the distances they traveled in the race, the days they were lost, the number of dogs on their teams and the number of pounds they lost.

THE CLUES

1. Helen, Hayley and Greg were all lost for more than 10 days, they all had more than 10 dogs on their teams, and they all lost more than 10 pounds.
2. The number 17 applied to Helen, Hayley and Greg one time each, the number 16 applied to Helen, Hayley and Greg one time each and, of course, the number 14 applied to Helen, Hayley and Greg one time each.
3. Helen traveled exactly 100 miles more than Hayley, and George traveled exactly 100 miles more than June.
4. The person who was lost the fewest days did not travel the shortest distance before dropping out.
5. Greg had twice as many dogs as George, and Helen lost twice as much weight as June.
6. Greg was not lost the most days and George was not lost the fewest days.

Helen	Hayley	Greg	George	June
800 miles	800 miles	800 miles	800 miles	800 miles
600 miles	600 miles	600 miles	600 miles	600 miles
500 miles	500 miles	500 miles	500 miles	500 miles
300 miles	300 miles	300 miles	300 miles	300 miles
200 miles	200 miles	200 miles	200 miles	200 miles
17 days	17 days	17 days	17 days	17 days
16 days	16 days	16 days	16 days	16 days
14 days	14 days	14 days	14 days	14 days
10 days	10 days	10 days	10 days	10 days
7 days	7 days	7 days	7 days	7 days
17 dogs	17 dogs	17 dogs	17 dogs	17 dogs
16 dogs	16 dogs	16 dogs	16 dogs	16 dogs
14 dogs	14 dogs	14 dogs	14 dogs	14 dogs
10 dogs	10 dogs	10 dogs	10 dogs	10 dogs
7 dogs	7 dogs	7 dogs	7 dogs	7 dogs
17 pounds	17 pounds	17 pounds	17 pounds	17 pounds
16 pounds	16 pounds	16 pounds	16 pounds	16 pounds
14 pounds	14 pounds	14 pounds	14 pounds	14 pounds
10 pounds	10 pounds	10 pounds	10 pounds	10 pounds
7 pounds	7 pounds	7 pounds	7 pounds	7 pounds

50 Selling Food

THE STORY

Bess, Baxter, Connie, Drake and Diane all owned sandwich shops. One recent day, they met and decided to have a contest to see who could sell the most hot dogs, burgers, milkshakes and colas in a single day. They sold 100, 95, 90, 80 and 75 hot dogs. They sold 100, 95, 90, 80 and 75 burgers. They sold 100, 95, 90, 80 and 75 milkshakes. They sold 100, 95, 90, 80 and 75 colas. Based on the clues, match the shop owners with the number of hot dogs, burgers, milkshakes and colas they sold on the day of the contest.

THE CLUES

1. Bess was the only person who was not first in one category and last in another category.
2. Bess sold exactly 5 more hot dogs than Baxter, and Connie sold exactly 5 more hot dogs than Drake but, of course, Connie did not sell the most hot dogs.
3. Baxter did not sell the fewest hot dogs, Baxter sold exactly 5 more burgers than Connie but, of course, Baxter did not sell the most burgers.
4. Diane sold exactly the same number of burgers and shakes, and Diane sold more burgers than Bess.
5. Bess sold exactly 5 more shakes than Baxter, and Connie sold exactly 5 more colas than Bess.

Bess	Baxter	Connie	Drake	Diane
100 hot dogs	100 hot dogs	100 hot dogs	100 hot dogs	100 hot dogs
95 hot dogs	95 hot dogs	95 hot dogs	95 hot dogs	95 hot dogs
90 hot dogs	90 hot dogs	90 hot dogs	90 hot dogs	90 hot dogs
80 hot dogs	80 hot dogs	80 hot dogs	80 hot dogs	80 hot dogs
75 hot dogs	75 hot dogs	75 hot dogs	75 hot dogs	75 hot dogs
100 burgers	100 burgers	100 burgers	100 burgers	100 burgers
95 burgers	95 burgers	95 burgers	95 burgers	95 burgers
90 burgers	90 burgers	90 burgers	90 burgers	90 burgers
80 burgers	80 burgers	80 burgers	80 burgers	80 burgers
75 burgers	75 burgers	75 burgers	75 burgers	75 burgers
100 shakes	100 shakes	100 shakes	100 shakes	100 shakes
95 shakes	95 shakes	95 shakes	95 shakes	95 shakes
90 shakes	90 shakes	90 shakes	90 shakes	90 shakes
80 shakes	80 shakes	80 shakes	80 shakes	80 shakes
75 shakes	75 shakes	75 shakes	75 shakes	75 shakes
100 colas	100 colas	100 colas	100 colas	100 colas
95 colas	95 colas	95 colas	95 colas	95 colas
90 colas	90 colas	90 colas	90 colas	90 colas
80 colas	80 colas	80 colas	80 colas	80 colas
75 colas	75 colas	75 colas	75 colas	75 colas

Answers

1. Timely Crows

Punky	Hinky	Pecky
90 feet	100 feet	80 feet
6 hrs. eating	4 hrs. eating	8 hrs. eating
4 hrs. raiding	8 hrs. raiding	6 hrs. raiding
8 hrs. chasing	6 hrs. chasing	4 hrs. chasing

2. Going Bananas

Bunky	Billy	Blinky
25 years old	20 years old	30 years old
75 pies	100 pies	25 pies
25 jelly	75 jelly	100 jelly
100 pudding	25 pudding	75 pudding

3. Fruit Counts

Sharon	Sammy	Sarah	Sherman
250 peaches	500 peaches	750 peaches	1,000 peaches
1,000 apples	750 apples	500 apples	250 apples
750 lemons	1,000 lemons	250 lemons	500 lemons
500 pears	250 pears	1,000 pears	750 pears

4. At Home With A Squirrel

Nutter	Buffy	Sammy	Louie
75 years old	100 years old	150 years old	50 years old
40 in. diameter	30 in. diameter	60 in. diameter	80 in. diameter
50 ft. tall	90 ft. tall	100 ft. tall	110 ft. tall
1,000 nuts	1,500 nuts	800 nuts	600 nuts

5. Your Turtles Are Numbered

Tara	Tilly	Tammy	Thomas
20 hat	15 hat	5 hat	10 hat
10 vest	5 vest	20 vest	15 vest
5 shirt	10 shirt	15 shirt	20 shirt
15 shorts	20 shorts	10 shorts	5 shorts

6. Too Much Work?

Glenview	Northbrook	Northfield	Deerfield
3,500 doctors	5,000 doctors	4,000 doctors	6,000 doctors
7,500 lawyers	8,000 lawyers	7,000 lawyers	6,000 lawyers
4,000 teachers	3,000 teachers	4,700 teachers	4,600 teachers
5,000 florists	4,500 florists	4,200 florists	4,300 florists

7. Watching Robins

Romeo	Richie	Robbie	Ruth
375 men	400 men	275 men	300 men
750 women	700 women	600 women	550 women
2,200 boys	2,100 boys	1,750 boys	2,000 boys
2,000 girls	2,300 girls	1,950 girls	1,925 girls

8. Farming Figures

Smith	Jones	Brown	White
150 wheat	200 wheat	100 wheat	75 wheat
200 corn	150 corn	75 corn	100 corn
100 soybeans	75 soybeans	200 soybeans	150 soybeans
75 beets	100 beets	150 beets	200 beets

9. I Get A Kick Out Of You

Ryan	Reggie	Rosa	Rub
80 uniform	90 uniform	75 uniform	40 uniform
500 shin	490 shin	470 shin	450 shin
300 ankle	315 ankle	320 ankle	325 ankle
71 head	65 head	77 head	74 head

10. And The Winner Is

Tom	Tess	Tillie	Timmy
60 years old	65 years old	50 years old	45 years old
4,500 speeches	4,700 speeches	4,900 speeches	5,000 speeches
$30,000	$27,000	$25,000	$20,000
15,000 votes	17,000 votes	20,000 votes	18,000 votes

11. The School Is Jumping

Glenn	Gloria	Gina	George	Gail
12 ft. broad	13 ft. broad	16 ft. broad	18 ft. broad	17 ft. broad
40 shot put	39 shot put	30 shot put	37 shot put	35 shot put
15 ft. vault	16 ft. vault	14 ft. vault	13 ft. vault	12 ft. vault

12. And The Eat Goes On

Jack	Jane	Junior	Josie	Jim
17 pizza	18 pizza	22 pizza	21 pizza	20 pizza
30 tacos	32 tacos	25 tacos	28 tacos	27 tacos
44 fish	42 fish	40 fish	34 fish	38 fish

13. Used Car Sales

Sam	Sharon	Sheila	Stan	Sophie
1960	1955	1949	1950	1953
97,500 mi.	95,000 mi.	94,500 mi.	93,500 mi.	92,000 mi.
150 HP	300 HP	400 HP	425 HP	450 HP

14. Pet Store Sales

Diane	Daisy	David	Dina	Darlene
600 puppies	500 puppies	1,200 puppies	800 puppies	700 puppies
800 birds	700 birds	500 birds	1,200 birds	600 birds
800 hamsters	700 hamsters	600 hamsters	500 hamsters	1,200 hamsters

15. Flower Power

Ben	Betty	Byron	Belle	Beverly
11,988 roses	11,400 roses	11,964 roses	11,940 roses	11,520 roses
9,480 daisies	9,600 daisies	9,216 daisies	9,228 daisies	9,240 daisies
6,600 posies	6,708 posies	7,200 posies	6,696 posies	6,660 posies

16. Bowling Numbers

Bert	Bill	Betsy	Bonnie	Bella
1st–280	1st–285	1st–300	1st–290	1st–270
2nd–190	2nd–160	2nd–100	2nd–195	2nd–180
3rd–130	3rd–155	3rd–200	3rd–115	3rd–150

17. Acme Corporation

A	B	C	D	E
9,600 widgets	9,900 widgets	9,400 widgets	9,000 widgets	10,000 widgets
2,000 gizmos	1,500 gizmos	1,980 gizmos	1,800 gizmos	1,700 gizmos
1,160 returns	1,140 returns	2,276 returns	2,160 returns	1,170 returns

18. Elephant Diets

Jimbo	Larry	Terry	Barry	Barney
45 age	30 age	50 age	65 age	60 age
2,150 weight	2,100 weight	2,050 weight	2,200 weight	2,580 weight
215 lost	420 lost	410 lost	220 lost	258 lost

19. Selling Farmers

Alice	Bret	Calvin	Doris	Ernie
1,100 corn	1,050 corn	1,090 corn	1,200 corn	1,250 corn
800 potatoes	850 potatoes	900 potatoes	845 potatoes	840 potatoes
1,400 tomatoes	1,425 tomatoes	1,390 tomatoes	1,500 tomatoes	1,450 tomatoes
775 beets	925 beets	800 beets	875 beets	900 beets

20. Restless Monkeys

Bingo	Gingo	Tinko	Dingo	Ringo
10 inches	14 inches	9 inches	7 inches	5 inches
80 seconds	90 seconds	70 seconds	60 seconds	58 seconds
90 feet	80 feet	72 feet	66 feet	75 feet
8 pints	10 pints	12 pints	16 pints	14 pints

21. What's Up Dock?

Salty	Nemo	Windy	Kirk	Cookie
50 ft. long	70 ft. long	45 ft. long	40 ft. long	29 ft. long
50 ft. mast	55 ft. mast	60 ft. mast	70 ft. mast	80 ft. mast
10,000 miles	9,998 miles	9,500 miles	9,450 miles	9,000 miles
70 days	65 days	80 days	90 days	85 days

22. Wood You Be Mine?

Willie	Wilma	Walt	Wallis	Waylon
21 ft. length	30 ft. length	28 ft. length	25 ft. length	20 ft. length
10 ft. width	7 ft. width	9 ft. width	8 ft. width	5 ft. width
400 nails	390 nails	370 nails	350 nails	300 nails
$4,000	$4,100	$4,250	$5,000	$4,500

23. Just Pottering Around

Peter	Patty	Penny	Paul	Pierre
90 cups	85 cups	80 cups	65 cups	70 cups
100 saucers	110 saucers	140 saucers	130 saucers	120 saucers
65 vases	70 vases	60 vases	50 vases	45 vases
50 inches	40 inches	30 inches	20 inches	25 inches

24. A Classy Picnic

Donna	Drake	Debra	Diane	David
12 boys	15 boys	17 boys	20 boys	18 boys
13 girls	11 girls	14 girls	16 girls	19 girls
70 hot dogs	90 hot dogs	95 hot dogs	100 hot dogs	80 hot dogs
180 glasses	100 glasses	160 glasses	140 glasses	200 glasses

25. Squat's Happening?

Eddie	Edris	Ellie	Eliot	Ernie
490 push-ups	480 push-ups	550 push-ups	525 push-ups	500 push-ups
1,100 sit-ups	1,000 sit-ups	900 sit-ups	1,050 sit-ups	980 sit-ups
125 pull-ups	150 pull-ups	100 pull-ups	70 pull-ups	90 pull-ups
270 squats	280 squats	290 squats	300 squats	295 squats

26. I Herd That

Alpha	Beta	Crown	Dofuss	Enid
300 elk	400 elk	1,000 elk	800 elk	500 elk
400 bison	300 bison	800 bison	500 bison	1,000 bison
1,000 reindeer	800 reindeer	500 reindeer	400 reindeer	300 reindeer
500 antelope	1,000 antelope	400 antelope	300 antelope	800 antelope

27. Amusement Parking

Chet	Carla	Carol	Champ	Celine
170 parks	185 parks	205 parks	215 parks	225 parks
1,000 roller	900 roller	800 roller	750 roller	700 roller
400 Ferris	300 Ferris	350 Ferris	375 Ferris	200 Ferris
2,500 m-g-r	2,250 m-g-r	2,000 m-g-r	1,250 m-g-r	1,000 m-g-r

28. Something Fishy

Victor	Vinnie	Val	Vera	Violet
1,000 shrimp	1,500 shrimp	1,450 shrimp	1,400 shrimp	1,300 shrimp
750 perch	500 perch	600 perch	700 perch	725 perch
1,500 tuna	3,000 tuna	2,800 tuna	2,000 tuna	2,900 tuna
400 flounder	100 flounder	200 flounder	300 flounder	350 flounder

29. Quadruple Play

Alvin	Alice	Arthur	Annie	Albert
7 France	8 France	9 France	10 France	12 France
10 England	12 England	9 England	8 England	7 England
8 Spain	7 Spain	9 Spain	12 Spain	10 Spain
12 Italy	10 Italy	9 Italy	7 Italy	8 Italy

30. Bling It On

Pierre	Pamela	Patrick	Paula	Peter
350 watches	300 watches	400 watches	450 watches	425 watches
420 earrings	460 earrings	500 earrings	440 earrings	475 earrings
850 rings	1,000 rings	700 rings	800 rings	900 rings
100 necklaces	70 necklaces	75 necklaces	50 necklaces	90 necklaces

31. It's A Hit!

Randy	Raul	Rita	Rick	Ruth
April 9,750	April 10,000	April 9,950	April 9,500	April 9,700
May 20,000	May 19,500	May 19,900	May 19,400	May 19,000
June 39,800	June 40,000	June 19,500	June 15,000	June 19,000
July 80,000	July 79,600	July 38,000	July 34,000	July 30,000

32. Save A Coin

Zack	Zelda	Zoe	Zoltan	Zorba
1,700 quarters	1,200 quarters	2,000 quarters	2,200 quarters	2,100 quarters
10,000 dimes	12,000 dimes	13,000 dimes	13,500 dimes	14,000 dimes
21,000 nickels	19,000 nickels	22,500 nickels	25,000 nickels	23,000 nickels
38,000 pennies	4,2000 pennies	45,000 pennies	46,000 pennies	50,000 pennies

33. Comb Again?

Teddy	Toula	Tammy	Terry	Tyree
10,200 feet	10,560 feet	7,200 feet	8,400 feet	9,000 feet
2,040 shells	2,160 shells	2,400 shells	1,800 shells	2,280 shells
900 stones	1,030 stones	1,140 stones	1,200 stones	630 stones
48 coins	40 coins	49 coins	50 coins	56 coins

34. Don't Toy With Me

Mike	Mabel	Mary	Mack	Myra
138 dolls	155 dolls	150 dolls	140 dolls	139 dolls
200 games	160 games	175 games	180 games	195 games
650 balls	575 balls	640 balls	630 balls	625 balls
35 puzzles	75 puzzles	50 puzzles	60 puzzles	70 puzzles

35. Spare No Expense

Alice	Amy	Annie	Ava	Arlene
$27,000 flowers	$23,000 flowers	$18,000 flowers	$22,000 flowers	$10,000 flowers
$22,000 dress	$18,000 dress	$23,000 dress	$27,000 dress	$10,000 dress
$23,000 food	$27,000 food	$22,000 food	$18,000 food	$10,000 food
$18,000 band	$22,000 band	$27,000 band	$23,000 band	$10,000 band

36. Swinging Shoppers

Jerry	Willie	Nicky	Calvin	Bogey
18 stores	15 stores	20 stores	22 stores	17 stores
81 pants	75 pants	79 pants	83 pants	80 pants
10 shoe pairs	27 shoe pairs	23 shoe pairs	19 shoe pairs	15 shoe pairs
58 shirts	40 shirts	45 shirts	30 shirts	55 shirts

37. De Sign! De Sign!

Nicky	Vickie	Claude	Patty	Pierre
80 yds. silk	85 yds. silk	90 yds. silk	100 yds. silk	75 yds. silk
90 yds. cotton	80 yds. cotton	85 yds. cotton	75 yds. cotton	100 yds. cotton
85 yds. satin	90 yds. satin	80 yds. satin	75 yds. satin	100 yds. satin
85 yds. linen	90 yds. linen	80 yds. linen	100 yds. linen	75 yds. linen

38. Library Business

Alpha	Beta	Crown	Dofuss	Enid
980 visitors	1,000 visitors	990 visitors	950 visitors	975 visitors
1,950 loans	1,960 loans	3,000 loans	2,500 loans	1,900 loans
9,750 overdue	9,500 overdue	9,900 overdue	9,000 overdue	9,800 overdue
475 signs	500 signs	450 signs	400 signs	300 signs

39. Video Business

Albert	Betty	Connie	Dwayne	Elvis
4,000 comedy	3,800 comedy	4,400 comedy	4,500 comedy	3,500 comedy
8,000 thriller	6,500 thriller	8,800 thriller	9,000 thriller	7,000 thriller
4,000 action	6,000 action	5,500 action	3,000 action	5,000 action
400 music	650 music	350 music	450 music	700 music

40. Time For A Change?

Goro	Harlow	Chico	Zero	Gino
90 rats	110 rats	200 rats	190 rats	150 rats
90 bats	130 bats	170 bats	160 bats	140 bats
50 cats	60 cats	75 cats	70 cats	65 cats
5 newts	10 newts	25 newts	20 newts	15 newts

41. Time Travels

Nate	Nancy	Neil	Nellie	Ned
age 30	age 35	age 38	age 40	age 39
year 3000	year 2990	year 2505	year 2400	year 2105
year 1750	year 1775	year 1800	year 1850	year 1900
1,250 total	1,215 total	705 total	550 total	205 total

42. Lumbering Along

Alice	Betty	Calvin	David	Eric
age 50	age 60	age 30	age 20	age 25
78 feet	75 feet	63 feet	84 feet	90 feet
68 in. tree	72 in. tree	36 in. tree	34 in. tree	30 in. tree
17 in. pancake	18 in. pancake	46 in. pancake	40 in. pancake	50 in. pancake

43. Town Rectangles

Alpha	Beta	Crown	Dofuss	Enid
276 ft. length	291 ft. length	282 ft. length	255 ft. length	300 ft. length
126 ft. width	150 ft. width	174 ft. width	99 ft. width	201 ft. width
3,864 sq. yds.	4,850 sq. yds.	5,452 sq. yds.	2,805 sq. yds.	6,700 sq. yds.
10 ft. tower	9 ft. tower	18 ft. tower	20 ft. tower	16 ft. tower

44. A Fortune In Cookies

Adams	Bates	Twain	Wilson	Taft
10,680 cookies	10,800 cookies	10,200 cookies	9,900 cookies	9,000 cookies
8,868 cupcake	9,120 cupcake	8,880 cupcake	8,808 cupcake	8,760 cupcake
7,740 doughnuts	7,776 doughnuts	7,680 doughnuts	7,668 doughnuts	7,620 doughnuts
3,720 brownies	3,780 brownies	3,756 brownies	3,696 brownies	3,600 brownies

45. School Nurses

Queenie	Retta	Sophie	Trudy	Vicky
260 bandages	270 bandages	150 bandages	200 bandages	250 bandages
420 lozenges	425 lozenges	400 lozenges	375 lozenges	415 lozenges
95 ice packs	90 ice packs	45 ice packs	80 ice packs	70 ice packs
40 squirts	35 squirts	25 squirts	15 squirts	30 squirts

46. Happy Webbing Day

Creeper	Leggy	Spot	Muffy	Fido
24 inches	18 inches	48 inches	36 inches	12 inches
850 flies	900 flies	450 flies	425 flies	700 flies
350 moths	225 moths	200 moths	100 moth	175 moths
85 bees	70 bees	90 bees	45 bees	30 bees

47. Jockey Careers

Tom	Jerry	Mutt	Jeff	Curley
4th place 40	5th place 50	3rd place 30	2nd place 20	1st place 10
5th place 50	4th place 40	3rd place 30	1st place 10	2nd place 20
1st place 10	2nd place 20	3rd place 30	5th place 50	4th place 40
2nd place 20	1st place 10	3rd place 30	4th place 40	5th place 50

48. Cone Heads

Alice	Belle	Carol	Dale	Evelyn
60 years old	70 years old	30 years old	35 years old	50 years old
4th in line	5th in line	1st in line	2nd in line	3rd in line
5 vanilla	3 vanilla	2 vanilla	1 vanilla	4 vanilla
5 peach	2 peach	3 peach	4 peach	1 peach

49. Sledding With Dogs

Helen	Hayley	Greg	George	June
300 miles	200 miles	800 miles	600 miles	500 miles
17 days	14 days	16 days	10 days	7 days
16 dogs	17 dogs	14 dogs	7 dogs	10 dogs
14 pounds	16 pounds	17 pounds	10 pounds	7 pounds

50. Selling Food

Bess	Baxter	Connie	Drake	Diane
95 hot dogs	90 hot dogs	80 hot dogs	75 hot dogs	100 hot dogs
90 burgers	80 burgers	75 burgers	100 burgers	95 burgers
80 shakes	75 shakes	100 shakes	90 shakes	95 shakes
90 colas	100 colas	95 colas	80 colas	75 colas